HELPING FOSTER CHILDREN IN SCHOOL

HELPING FOSTER CHILDREN IN SCHOOL

A Guide for Foster Parents,
Social Workers and Teachers

JOHN DEGARMO
FOREWORD BY HAROLD SLOKE

Jessica Kingsley *Publishers*
London and Philadelphia

First published in 2015
by Jessica Kingsley Publishers
73 Collier Street
London N1 9BE, UK
and
400 Market Street, Suite 400
Philadelphia, PA 19106, USA

www.jkp.com

Library of Congress Cataloging in Publication Data
DeGarmo, John, 1969-
 Helping foster children in school : a guide for foster parents, social workers and
teachers / John
DeGarmo.
   pages cm
 Includes bibliographical references and index.
 ISBN 978-1-84905-745-5 (alk. paper)
 1. Foster children--Education--United States. 2. Children with social disabilities--
Education--United
States. 3. Youth with social disabilities--Education--United States. 4. Foster children-
-Services for--
United States. I. Title.
 LC4091.D44 2015
 371.826'94--dc23
                                   2015002889

British Library Cataloguing in Publication Data
A CIP catalogue record for this book is available from the British Library

ISBN 978 1 84905 745 5
eISBN 978 1 78450 162 4

Printed and bound in the United States

For Brandon, Garret, and Preston; three brothers who came to live with me, and reminded me of the importance of education for all children in foster care.

Train a child in the way he should go, and
when he is old he will not turn from it.

Proverbs 22:6

CONTENTS

Foreword

Harold Sloke

I wake up in the middle of the night to a smack across my face. I then feel my eight-year-old body flying across the room. My mother is screaming and pleading with my stepfather to stop. He picks me up by my throat and proceeds to tell me I will turn out to be a failure just like my father. "Shut up, woman!" he yells as he slaps her across the face. "You want a reason to cry??? I'll give you a reason to cry!" He then goes into the other room to grab his 12 gauge shotgun. He tells me to get on my knees and he puts the gun to my head. "Here's your reason to cry. He's better off dead anyway," he tells my mother. The only question I can ask myself is what can save me? Will it be like this forever?

My early childhood was the scariest time of my life. Not necessarily because of the abuse, but because of the uncertainty of my future. My mother and stepfather would often tell me about their own childhood horror stories, as they were both abused and neglected also. All I knew was that I didn't want to repeat that cycle. But what could save me? I did not have that answer during that time. Instead, I read whole sets of encyclopedias and my Bible over and over again as I was nailed shut into my room. My meals were given to me underneath my door. I missed many days of school because they did not want others to see the bruises. I hoped that better days would come. What could possibly save me?

When I entered the foster care system at the age of 13, I was already involved with the juvenile justice system. I joined a gang for protection and for a sense of family. I was certainly aware that I was not heading down the right road, but at the moment I did not care. I was free from the abuse of my mother and stepdad.

Instead, I found myself in a new type of hell. Before I aged out of the foster care system at the age of 18, I had been in over 30 foster homes, group homes, and juvenile placements. This resulted in me attending 12 high schools. With each school move, my credits failed to transfer. I found myself repeating ninth grade for the third time. On my second day in my eleventh high school, I laid my head on my desk in my keyboarding class. I was feeling quite depressed that day and my teacher, Karen Parker, noticed it. She asked me what was wrong and I told her a little about my situation. She genuinely seemed to care, so I slowly told her more. She was shocked that I was still in the ninth grade and that none of my credits had transferred. She advocated on my behalf until I received enough credits to almost be in the eleventh grade. I eventually graduated high school at the age of 19 with a 1.8 GPA. The Grade Point Average ranges from 0.0 to 4.0, so a 1.8 GPA is considered pretty low.

I joined the Army Reserves after graduation and went off to active duty for about a year. When I returned, I enrolled into a community college since I could not get into a university with such a low high school GPA. In 2012, I applied and was accepted to the Congressional Coalition on Adoption Institute Foster Youth Internship. As a part of the internship, I had to write a policy report on how I would change the foster care system. I wrote about my educational experience in high school where my credits were not transferring over. My policy report transformed into the Uninterrupted Scholars Act, which amended the Family Educational Rights and Privacy Act to allow social workers to access foster children's educational records with each school transition in a timely manner. My story was featured nationally in the media. I worked on Capitol Hill for a while as a legislative aide. I never imagined during my childhood that I would make such a profound difference in others' lives.

I often give credit to Karen Parker for being my advocate and saving me. However, I never thought about it on a deeper level, until I was at the University of South Carolina Children's Law Center Conference as a keynote speaker in 2013. The main focus of the conference was educational outcomes for vulnerable youth. As I was telling my story, I looked at the crowd with tears in my eyes and said slowly, "My education saved me!" It was at that point I realized how far my education had taken me. Without graduating high school, I would have never been able to join the Army. My chances of employment would have been poor and I would have most likely continued a life of crime. It took only one person to believe in me and push me to the finish line when the odds seemed impossible.

I am currently a semester away from graduating with three bachelor degrees: a Bachelor of Social Work, a Bachelor of Science in Criminology and Criminal Justice, and a Bachelor of Arts in Political Science. I currently have a 3.957 GPA and am attending college on a full ride merit scholarship. I plan to obtain both a law degree and a PhD before I am 30 years old. I am in love with learning and furthering my education. It has made such a huge difference in my life and I could not imagine my life without an education. It only takes one Karen Parker to make a difference in a foster child's life. Pushing foster children toward education is the greatest investment one can make in the foster care system, as education helps transform vulnerable youth to become influential, driven, inspirational, self-reliant leaders.

Harold Sloke
https://rjsloke.wordpress.com

ACKNOWLEDGMENTS

I would like to thank the many foster parents and social workers I have worked with over the years, as I have traveled across the nation. I am so thankful for what you do. It is with your encouragement that I continue to train others, and write this book. I also would like to thank my wife, Dr. Kelly DeGarmo, as she continues to not only teach our own foster children how to read and write, but also continues to love and care for them as her own.

Introduction

When I first began teaching, and before I was a foster parent, I knew very little about foster care, or about foster children. In fact, what I thought I knew about children in foster care, and about the foster care system, was as far from the truth as possible. Like most of the general public, I had false ideas and beliefs about foster children, and much of it was negative. This was due mainly to the false stereotypes that abound in society. As a result, I was not prepared to meet the many desperate needs of the students from foster homes in my classroom. Even further, after all my years of college, and with additional instructional workshops, I did not have the training required to best help foster children as they struggled in my classroom, and neither did my colleagues.

After a few foster children had passed through my own home, I began to appreciate the fact that I had to not only adjust my teaching habits for foster children, but I also had to become my own foster children's advocate at their schools. I watched my foster children struggle in my fellow teachers' classrooms, and also was witness to these same teachers as they failed to understand the various emotional challenges the children in my home were going through on a daily basis. Indeed, there were times when I had to politely intervene on behalf of my foster child. There were also times when I had to sit across the table from a fellow teacher as we discussed how my foster child's behavior was interfering in the classroom setting. My desire to better assist both my colleagues and foster children led to my doctoral studies on the subject. I simply wanted to help foster children succeed in school, as well as bring awareness about their struggles to our schools.

Foster children, in general, tend to perform below average in regard to both academic performance and positive behavior compared with those students who come from traditional homes as well as children from economically disadvantaged homes. The majority of children under foster care supervision experience problems in behavior while enrolled in public schools. Those foster children who were taken from homes due to neglect repeatedly suffer from a number of developmental delays. These include poor language and vocabulary development, thus impairing communication skills.

Since foster children are often behind academically, as well as struggle with the fact that they are coming from outside school districts with different expectations, teachers in a foster child's school need to be conscious of this fact. Foster children struggle with many personal and emotional issues while in the foster home, and homework is often not the main objective while in the home each evening. Instead, the emotional issues a child faces may take center stage on a particular evening. Foster parents need to let their child's teacher know this, and ask that they cooperate. Teachers need to assign homework with this in mind, being sensitive to the children's issues. It is important for foster parents to meet with the teachers, the school counselor, and perhaps even an administrator of the school when enrolling the foster child, and explain these concerns to them. Like I was beforehand, it is highly likely that they have not had much experience with foster children, nor the challenges they face.

As a foster parent, you will need to reach out to the teachers, and ask for as much information and updates as possible. It is essential to your child's success in school that you become actively involved and interested in your child's school life. Look for ways to volunteer in the school. Encourage your foster child to become active in after-school activities. Take an interest in your child's school work, and make sure it is done to the best of his or her ability each evening. Help your child study, and praise them when they do well. If you have a young foster child in the early years of school, read to them each evening, or listen to them read to you. Help them with their spelling and writing skills. Quite simply, be your foster child's advocate with their teachers, and in their school.

Each chapter in this book begins with a personal observation about the chapter's topic from a foster parent, or someone who has worked with foster parents. These personal observations offer insight into the foster care system from those who have lived it on a day-to-day basis, and who have experienced the joys, the sorrows, and the challenges of working with foster children. By reading through these observations, you will be able to gain valuable insight into fostering beyond what any training session or publication might suggest. The Appendix contains new foster student protocol and team meeting templates that can be photocopied for personal use.

As I write this, school is about to begin in my area. I have already met with the teachers of the two foster children currently living in my home. Fortunately, these teachers have already taught many of the foster children who my wife and I have been blessed to have in our home over the years, and these teachers and I have been able to build a healthy working partnership, through both good times and bad. It is only with the combined effort of the foster parent, the child's teachers, and the social worker that the foster child has a chance for success in school.

Dr. John DeGarmo

CHAPTER 1

Foster Care
An Introduction

The numbers are dire. The desire is there, but as long as there has been foster care there has been severe deficiency in the education of those who find themselves in the care of someone other than the biological parents. Not to say that those from the traditional nuclear family walk to the graduation stage without any hurdles to jump over, but you'd be hard pressed to find anyone in or out of the world of child welfare who would argue against foster youth being the first to suffer when it comes to education.

My story of education isn't that far away from what every other foster kid goes through. When I went to care, it meant I was leaving my school as well. At that point I was finishing my freshman year of high school, so far along that moving to the next grade was done with ease. I hopped through a couple of homes and with them a couple of schools. I landed in a pretty nice foster home and a pretty nice school district but the family decided to move towns, taking me with them. A new house and a new school.

Unlike most foster youth my school records followed me everywhere I went. I was fortunate not to lose any credits or suffer any penalties, though I did lose the eligibility to participate in sports due to all the moves. I made due. I played intramural basketball and found a home in the yearbook department. Unlike a lot of foster youth, I'm pretty outgoing, I acclimate well. It wasn't too difficult for me to settle in, make some friends, and enjoy the stability of being in school for more than a year.

But the stability ended and, like most foster youth, reality started. Two weeks before graduation I aged out of foster care. I moved in with my girlfriend, prepared to finish school and figure out the next step. I was shocked when I was called into the Vice Principal's office. The whole thing seemed to move in slow motion. I was asked what my living situation was. I explained that I had aged out and moved into a new home in the school district. I was asked if I paid rent. I responded with a no. I was asked if I paid any utilities or had any house bills in my name. I had lived there all of two days so, again, the answer was no. I was then informed that since I could not prove that I lived in the school district, it was the position of the school that I be expelled.

I was two weeks away. I was two weeks away from a cap and gown. I was two weeks away from awkwardly laughing with the rest of my class over embarrassing memories created in the halls. I was two weeks away from a tassel that would hang from my rearview mirror for the first year of college. I was two weeks away from being able to remember the year I graduated high school. But I didn't get those things. I confuse the last year of high school all the time. I almost never get it right.

Instead I got to fill up my best friend's car with everything I had at the school. A few days later I would fill that car again with everything I owned. The girl moved out of state. I was diploma-less and for the moment homeless. I had direction a few days earlier, I had a plan. Now I was standing outside a house I couldn't live in, a school that had shut me out, and a future that looked very bleak.

I lucked out though. My best friend's mom saw my things in her son's car and started asking questions. Before I knew it she had me taking a General Educational Development course and enrolled in the local state university affiliate college with an apartment I shared with her son.

Not every kid in care has that person looking out for them. In fact, very few have the support necessary to make it in the real world, let alone college. Numbers don't lie. Only seven percent of foster youth achieve an Associate's Degree. I didn't, college was too much fun for someone like me, grades suffered. And a measly three percent of foster youth ever see the sheepskin of a Bachelor's Degree.

Take a moment to grasp that fact. In any given year there are nearly 400,000 kids in foster care. Of that number 20,000 will age out. Of that number, *half* will be homeless. And somewhere in all that muck, the three percenters and seven percenters find their way. What an amazing achievement that is...for them.

The rest will suffer through. The lack of resources, or knowledge of those resources, will baffle and frustrate them. They will give up. For some the call of immediate income will be too much to pass up, leading them straight into the workforce.

Some will turn to the military, some will turn to crime, and some will be lost forever.

There are programs out there for foster youth to further their education. Scholarships, grants, federal programs that can help them make their way. You have a great guide through all the details.

When I started the nation's only monthly foster care magazine (I told you I landed on my feet) I sought qualified, informed members of the child welfare world. I found Dr. John DeGarmo. I prefer writers who practice what they preach. I find the articles are more informative, more passionate, and more genuine. Doc DeGarmo is the real deal. The man's house is always full of children. Children from care, children who have been adopted, and members of the DeGarmo tribe all live in harmony under one roof. That would be more than enough to fill one man's plate but the good Doctor still finds time to advocate, to educate, and to learn. The thing I like most about him is his relentless pursuit of education and educating those who are responsible for the educating of America's youth. A foster parent with an academic background who cares about the kids he cares for? I can get behind that.

There's no quick fix to the problems that face America's foster youth. Yet, there is hope. Moreover, efforts are being made every year to ensure the futures of the nation's foster youth. What is needed is more information. More sharing of ideas that work, programs that work, people who are making a difference. Dr. John DeGarmo is a great voice to add to the conversation. Both his personal experience as an educated member of the child welfare community and as a strong advocate who is passionate about educating and informing people about foster care. I think you are really going to enjoy this book.

So get started.

CHRIS CHMIELEWSKI
OWNER/EDITOR/FORMER FOSTER KID
FOSTER FOCUS MAGAZINE

The number of children in the United States being placed within a foster home continues at a high rate as the nation travels further into the twenty-first century. As of 2009, there were approximately 463,000 children in the United States who were placed within homes under the foster care system (U.S. Department of Health and Human Services 2010). Seventy-five percent of these foster children are of school age, with the average age of a foster child being 10 years of age (Child Welfare League of America [CWLA] 2005).

When children are placed into foster care, lives are often changed very quickly. No longer do they live with parents and family or are surrounded by people they know. Instead, they are, most often quite quickly, placed in a home with strangers and are no longer in touch with those they know or with whom they are familiar. Indeed, those who are in foster care have significant difficulties in school performance and adjustment to developmental tasks of adolescence. These difficulties often lead to additional problems later on in their lives.

For many children placed in foster care, a new school environment is thrust upon them. Foster children are often taken from their homes suddenly and without any notice, and placed in a foster home in a nearby county. As a result, a number of issues arise for the foster child, as they are faced with a new home and an unfamiliar environment. To begin with, foster children typically have low attendance rates, as they are moved from one home to another. This includes not only to their original foster home, but to other foster homes as well. During these transitions, children placed in child welfare agencies often miss a great deal of school, as their foster parents and social workers attend to duties such as enrolling the child into school, meeting with counselors and psychologists, and giving the child time to adequately adjust to the new living situation. Often, the child has difficulty registering in a new school, as well as ensuring that all transcript information remains current. In fact, teachers are often not aware that a foster child is placed in their classroom. Indeed, school counselors or administrators might not have this information, either.

As foster children come with a myriad of emotional issues, many teachers are simply not equipped to handle these issues. Foster children may lash out in the middle of class due to the unfamiliarity and instability of their life at that present time, and many teachers do not have the training or the resources to recognize and deal with these challenges. Along with this, foster children often have difficulty with trust issues when it comes to adults, as well as building a healthy relationship with an adult figure. Thus, the relationships between teachers and foster children are quite often unhealthy ones.

Teachers, as well as school counselors, do not often have the background information they might need when having a foster child under their supervision. In most cases, the background information is not permitted to be released due to issues of confidentiality through legal acts of protection. Yet, this information is necessary in order for a teacher to fully understand the student's needs and abilities. The more information a teacher has on the child, the better equipped the teacher becomes when trying to aid the child in his or her behavior and academic performance.

As the sudden move from a familiar home to an unfamiliar one can be a traumatic experience, children in foster care often struggle with a wide range of overwhelming emotions as they face being separated from family and loved ones, along with the difficulty of adjusting to a new home, foster family, and an environment that is foreign to them and not of their choosing. Along with this lies the concern of the foster child's mental health, as the new environment and the situation the child has been placed in creates the risk of disturbing and disrupting it.

Foster children often have a difficult time with exhibiting proper school behavior during the school day. For many of the children, school is a constant reminder that they are, indeed, foster children without a true home. The continuous reminder that their peers are living with biological family members while they are not is a difficult reality for them, and can be manifested in several ways. Some foster children simply withdraw and become antisocial, in an attempt to escape their current environment and world they have been thrust into. For many foster children, violent behavior becomes the norm, as they not only act out in a negative and disruptive fashion in the school, but in their foster home, too, prompting yet another move to another foster home and another school.

The foster care system is one that is not only complex, but also one that is not well known by the general public, or to school teachers. It is necessary to understand the system in order to grasp the difficulties that all foster children undergo in foster care. It is also important to appreciate the difficulties faced by foster parents, teachers, and social workers who work alongside the foster youth on a daily basis, both inside and outside schools.

A brief history of foster care in the United States

In order to fully understand the foster care system in the United States, it is necessary to look as far back as the eighteenth century. At that time, local government officials were given the task of distributing relief to the poor and impoverished. Often, these officials were also granted authority to indenture children from families in poverty in lieu of monetary relief. Local officials were to ensure that children were fed, housed, clothed, and provided the necessary training of skills. As society became more aware of the challenges of underprivileged children, along with the growing number of orphans, orphanages were established.

The early nineteenth century saw the establishment of what grew to become the middle class. At the same time, the conception grew that early childhood was an important and separate part of human development. The character of children was to be shaped by internalizing beliefs of morality and behavior rather than breaking their wills, the prevailing approach in colonial times. The outcome was a change in child-rearing methods, as children began to live longer and stay home for longer periods of time, instead of being forced to enter the workforce at early ages. The early nineteenth century was also a time that children only from low-income homes were indentured. Some states were required to furnish children a minimum of three months of education per year. As states began to wane in indenturing children by the middle of the nineteenth century, religious institutes, along with charitable organizations, began to open their own orphanages.

The year 1853 witnessed a drastic change in regard to orphans and impoverished children. Charles Loring Brace, an austere critic of orphanages and asylums, introduced the idea of placing these children in homes, rather than the traditional orphanage. Brace founded the Children's Aid Society (CAS) later in that year, with the vision that children should be placed in homes rather than in institutions. It was Brace's personal belief that children should live in rural areas, as he was against city life. As a result, Brace endeavored to place children from urban slums into homes in the country. Then 1873 saw Mary Ellen Wilson enter the scene. This young girl was found by a church worker when she was reported by her neighbors. Young Mary Ellen was bruised, thin, and her skin was caked in dirt. When a New York judge became aware of the situation, Mary Ellen was removed from her home, and placed into another, thus making her the first official foster child.

The later part of the nineteenth century saw an awareness of the importance of social issues, such as child abuse and parental neglect. The Society for the Prevention of Cruelty to Children (SPCC) was created and became active in large eastern cities. Soon, members of the SPCC were granted permission from the courts to remove children from abusive and neglectful homes and place them within other homes and orphan asylums. Families, such as those in Boston, Massachusetts, that took children into their homes were being paid. With this change in policy in payment to families, child placement agencies began to look more closely at the conditions in the placement homes where children were boarded. The term "foster care" came into fashion, sometimes replacing the phrase "boarding out."

In 1909, the White House Council of Children established a resolution that altered the earlier philosophy and policies in regard to child welfare. This resolution was a new philosophy that held the belief that children needed to be reared in happy and stable environments. Shortly after in 1915, California licensed, as well as regulated, agencies that found placement homes for children. Five years later, the state began to pay these homes for this service.

The Aid to Dependent Children (ADC) Act, which was Title IV of the Social Security Act, gave impoverished families access to federal funds, enabling these families to keep their children at home, rather than have the children placed in orphan asylums. Furthermore, the ADC, with its additional federal funding, aided those establishments that housed children taken from their homes. By 1950, more children were in foster homes than in orphanages and other institutions. The number of children in foster homes continued to increase so that, by 1960, there were twice as many children placed in foster homes than institutions. This number tripled by 1968, and by 1976, the number of children placed into foster homes exceeded 100,000.

A number of critics harshly criticized the foster care system, declaring that the ease in which children entered into care was troublesome. As a result of their heavy criticism, Congress passed federal foster care legislation, the Adoption Assistance and Child Welfare Act of 1980. This act addressed two critical issues. The first was that states resorted consistently to foster care as a means of intervention in regard to the child's relationship with the family. Second, the government saw placing children into foster care as an answer to the ever-growing dilemma of where to place children living outside of their homes. With this in mind, Congress expected the states to keep children safely in their own homes by using the states' own methods, resources, and other services.

Although the number of foster children placed in homes declined between the 1970s and the early 1980s, the number increased greatly beginning in the mid-1980s. From 1987 to 1992 the population of foster children went from 280,000 to more than 460,000. In addition, the number of children raised by their grandparents outside of foster care, or children living outside of their birth parents' yet in a relative's home, rose from two million to three million. In 1997, Congress passed the Adoption and Safe Families Act (ASFA). ASFA mandated that federal and local officials were responsible to create a program to focus on the nation's burgeoning foster care population, and that both federal and local officials were to focus principally on the reduction of time children spent in foster care.

Today, the foster care system faces tremendous cuts in budget, from state to state, and across the nation. Social workers are overworked and underpaid, and departments are understaffed. Yet, the number of foster children continues to increase throughout the country. Perhaps it is time to look more to the past in order to determine how the nation's child welfare agencies might best respond to the challenges of today, and of the future.

Foster care

Foster care is a form of placement for children who are in need of being placed in a home or environment outside of their home of origin. As foster care is intended to be a temporary placement, the time frame in a foster home varies from one foster child to the next. The average amount of time a foster child spends in the foster care system is 28.6 months, with half of all foster children being placed in another home for a year or more (CWLA 2005). As a result, most of these children have not experienced a stable or nurturing environment during their early, formative years (American Academy of Pediatrics 2000).

Children are placed under foster care for a number of reasons. Many of these reasons overlap, with the child suffering from numerous mental and emotional challenges (American Academy of Pediatrics 2000). Indeed, Takayama, Wolfe, and Coulter (1998) document that 51 percent of children placed into care come from homes of parents with substance abuse, with 15 percent of these parents also being incarcerated. Four percent of the parents are diagnosed with a psychiatric illness (Takayama *et al.* 1998). Thirty percent of foster children are taken from their homes due to neglect, while it was found that 25 percent of children suffered from physical and sexual abuse (Takayama *et al.* 1998). Along with this, 24 percent of children were living in conditions where there was no caregiver or were simply abandoned by family members (Takayama *et al.* 1998). Sixty percent of all foster children were also found to have suffered from health-related problems (Takayama *et al.* 1998). In general, 94 percent of all children in foster care suffer from some sort of physical health problem (Leslie *et al.* 2003).

Placement in the foster care system takes many forms. Some children may live with foster parents unrelated to them, while other children may live with relatives temporarily or with family members intent upon adopting the child. Over two million children live with family members outside of the foster care system, such as in group homes, or with family friends (CWLA 2005). Still other foster children may reside within groups or residential treatment centers (Evans and Armstrong 1994; Grogan-Kaylor 2000), or even in an intensive form known as

Treatment Foster Care, which provides therapeutic treatment services (Meadowcroft, Thomlison, and Chamberlain 1994).

When a child is placed in custody under foster care, the intention is for the child to eventually be reunited with his/her birth family. In 2005, 54 percent of all children leaving the foster system were reunited with birth parents or family members (CWLA 2005). Yet, findings suggest that children who are reunited with their parents face greater negative outcomes than those children who are not reunited with their family (Taussig, Clyman, and Landsverk 2001; Wulczyn 2004).

Children are taken into foster care custody only when a local child welfare agency, along with the courts, has determined that the current living conditions and parental care are unsuitable and harmful for the child's wellbeing (Marcus 1991). Of the 513,000 children under foster care supervision in 2005, 61 percent were white children, 15 percent were black, 17 percent were Hispanic, 1 percent was American Indian, 3 percent were Asian, and 4 percent were a combination of two or more races. Males made up the majority, with 52 percent (CWLA 2005).

Foster youth and teens

Foster care is available for any child from birth until 18 years of age, at which time most exit the foster system. The average age of a child in custody is 10.2 years, as of 2006, with 7.5 years of age the median age of the child entering into custody, and 9.5 years the median age of the child upon leaving the system, as of 2006 (Adoption and Foster Care Analysis and Reporting System [AFCARS] 2009). Of all children in foster care, 47 percent are in their teens (Massinga and Pecora 2004).

The placement of a child into your foster home is a life changing experience for a foster child. Placement disruption is the term used when a child is removed from a home and placed into the custody of a child welfare agency, and thus into a foster home. For many, it is a frightening time, as the fear of the unknown can quickly overwhelm a child. Others are filled with anger, as they emotionally reject the idea of being separated from their family members. Feelings of guilt may also arise within the foster child, as the child may believe that he or she may have had something to do with the separation from the birth and/or foster family. Some children experience self-doubt, as they feel that they simply did not deserve to stay with their family. For all, it is a traumatic experience that will forever alter the lives of foster children.

Many psychologists state that it is necessary for young children to form a relationship with at least one main parental figure or caregiver in order for the child to develop socially and emotionally. Yet, the removal of a child from his or her home, and placement into another's home through foster care, often makes this a difficult, traumatic experience. Often, the removal of a child from a home occurs after a caseworker has gathered evidence and presented this evidence to a court, along with the recommendation that the child be removed. Indeed, most foster care placements are made through the court system.

Those who are in foster care can have significant difficulties in school performance and adjustment to developmental tasks of adolescence (Harden 2004). These difficulties often lead to additional problems later on in their lives. In a demographic survey conducted by Courtney *et al.* (2001) of teens who were once placed under foster care supervision, 27 percent of males and 10 percent of females had been incarcerated at some time. Furthermore, their work revealed that 33 percent were receiving public assistance from the government, 37 percent had quit high school before graduating, and 50 percent were unemployed. Finally, the study revealed that 30 percent of former foster children were homeless.

Children are placed under foster care for a number of reasons. Many of these reasons overlap, with the child suffering from numerous mental and emotional challenges. These reasons may include one or more of the following:

- *Neglect:* A child may be neglected in a number of ways. A parent may neglect a child's basic need for food. Sanitary living conditions may be neglected, leaving a child in an unsanitary household. The lack of proper and needed medical conditions can also be a symptom of neglect. Children may face neglect due to lack of supervision, placing the child in an unsafe environment. Finally, many foster children suffer from emotional neglect, as their emotional needs are not met by a parent or adult.

- *Physical abuse:* Abuse takes many forms. One of these is the abuse through a physical injury caused by a parent or caregiver. Physical abuse also may take many forms, with the severity of the injury sustained ranging from a visible bruising to a more tragic situation where the parent or caregiver physically assaults the child. Physical abuse can even take the form of locking a child in a closet or other confined space. Often, the child welfare agency works with the parents in an attempt to help them learn alternative methods of discipline. However, when these methods fail, and a child becomes abused, the state steps in, removing the child from the household.

- *Sexual abuse:* Disturbingly so, sexual abuse also may take several different forms. Sexual abuse of a child may involve voyeurism, the viewing of pornographic material, or sexual acts with a child, or the act of sexual fondling, penetration, or rape.

- *Parental drug/alcohol abuse:* Those parents who abuse drugs and/or alcohol place their children in danger. This danger may result in neglect, physical abuse, or domestic violence.

- *Child drug/alcohol abuse:* Those parents who allow their child to take drugs and/or alcohol also place their children in danger. Parents may either ignore the danger or are unaware of the child's abuse of the drugs/alcohol.

- *Domestic violence:* When a child is living in an environment where two or more caregivers are engaged in a violent altercation, the child's safety is then jeopardized through this violence.

- *Inadequate housing:* When a parent is no longer able to provide a clean, safe, healthy environment for a child, the child is removed and placed into foster care. Many times, these children are homeless.

- *Incarceration:* Children may be placed into foster care after all parents or caregivers are unavailable due to their placement into prison.

- *Death:* On very rare occasions, a parent's death leads to a situation where there are no family members willing, able, or available to provide and care for a child.

- *Abandonment:* Abandonment occurs when a parent or caregiver chooses to leave the child voluntarily. Often, this abandonment may occur with a friend, neighbor, or baby sitter. Other times, a parent may simply leave the child at home for a great length of time.

Placement in the foster care system takes many forms. Some children may live with foster parents unrelated to them, while other children may live with relatives temporarily or with family members intent upon adopting the child. Over two million children live with family members outside of the foster care system, such as in group homes, or with family friends. Still other foster children may reside within groups or residential treatment centers, or even in an intensive form known as Treatment Foster Care, which provides therapeutic treatment services.

Visitations

Visitations are those scheduled, face-to-face meetings between a foster child and the biological parents or family members. These visitations are considered by many to be the main factor in bringing reunification between the child and parents, the end goal for foster parenting. Meetings are held in a central and neutral location, for example a community park, a church, or a child welfare agency. During this meeting, the social worker has the opportunity to assess the foster child's relationship with their parents or family members, and determine how the parents are progressing in their level of readiness for possible reunification. Visitations also provide the opportunity for parents to practice parenting skills, which the social worker will also assess. Those parents who do attend visitations on a regular and consistent basis are more likely to be reunified with their child.

For foster children, visitations have many positive attributes. To begin with, the foster child's visit with birth parents or other biological family members will likely reduce his or her sense of abandonment by them. Hopefully, the child's sense of self-worth and importance will be bolstered, as he or she feels reassurance by the birth parents that they continue to love the child, something that he or she may very well doubt and struggle with internally. By expressing these feelings, the child may continue to heal emotionally. The birth parents may also reassure the child that they are in a good home, and that they need to listen to the foster parents, and follow their rules, thus strengthening their own relationship with the foster family. In fact, those children who visit with their birth parents on a regular basis are less likely to exhibit behavioral problems at home and in school, as their level of anxiety decreases as they become better adjusted to placement within the family.

At times, visitations can be times of confusion and dread, for both the foster child and the foster parents. It can be most heart-wrenching for a foster child to arrive at a central location for visitation, only to wait for birth parents never to show. Other foster children may meet with their parents, yet have them speak negatively about the foster parents. Some may struggle with feelings of loyalty to both the foster parents and the birth parents. Still other foster children may be given false hope from their family members, hope about imminent reunification. Many of these foster children will return to their foster homes confused, frustrated, depressed, or full of anxiety. Misbehavior may increase in the home, as well as in school, as the child struggles to understand their parents' behavior. As a result, some foster parents, social workers, and even teachers, come to dread visitations as they feel they have to pick up the emotional pieces from the visits, or, for some, start from the beginning with the foster child.

Foster parents

Foster parents are those people who open their homes to foster children in an attempt to assist the troubled children. These licensed caregivers must go through a number of hours of training, attend orientation meetings, have their homes approved by the agency, and obtain a criminal background check. There are a number of challenges a foster parent faces when having a foster child placed in the home. Schofield and Beek (2005) suggested the following challenges: (a) promoting trust, (b) promoting authority, (c) promoting self-esteem, (d) promoting family membership, and (e) promoting autonomy; while Massinga and Pecora (2004) found challenges including (a) providing a secure base and home, (b) understanding and dealing with the child's behavior, (c) understanding and dealing with the child's thinking and feelings, and (d) working with the social worker.

Social workers

A social worker is an employee of the child welfare agency who is assigned to the foster child, generally for the entire time the child is placed under the care of the agency (K. Lanier, personal communication, May 21, 2010). The social worker selects a foster home placement for the child, attempting to find the best suitable home situation for both the foster child and the foster parent. Foster children are often enrolled in a new school when assigned a social worker to assist them in the foster care process. Eventual reunification with their parents and family is the hoped-for goal (Falke 1995). Social workers are specifically trained to provide mental health relief, as they often work with troubled children. They ensure that the medical needs of the child are met.

Social workers often deal with children who have serious behavioral problems, and those children who are emotionally depressed due to the situation they are in. They may also have to work with angry birth parents who blame the child welfare agency, or even the social workers themselves, for the removal of their child, or for their own personal issues.

However, difficult working conditions, poor compensation, larger caseloads due to reductions in staff, and the responsibilities of providing continuous support to the birth parents, foster children, and foster parents result in 22 percent of social workers failing to continue employment in this line of work past the first year, according to a county Department of Family and Children's (DFCS) social worker (K. Lanier, personal communication, May 21, 2010).

CHAPTER 2

Placement Disruptions

Dread filled my heart as 3:30 rolled around and I anticipated still another evening of homework! We had accepted a placement four months earlier of a sibling group of two who had been severely sexually abused by family members. The brother and sister were beautiful children and very needy! Each struggled in school, not because they were slow mentally, but because they were unable to focus.

Each afternoon we sat at the kitchen table where I spent 1–2 ½ hours encouraging, prodding, and pleading until we either set it aside to finish later or we completed the assignment. The finished product usually had holes in the paper from the eraser or sentences printed too large for the page, but at least we were done!

These children, like most foster children, had been so traumatized they were unable to focus and acted a lot like special needs children. Our home was the second home since leaving their birth family and depression was apparent in both children. We met with the teachers several times and corresponded by e-mail, notes, and phone. We all wanted to see these kids succeed! But...

How do you explain to a teacher why this child steals, lies, wets his pants, makes weird noises under his breath, and then runs up and hands you a paper with a picture drawn of a heart with "Mom, I really love you!" printed on it?

How do you explain the reason for the nightmares and constant crying or the tattling and wanting more hugs? After working in child care for over 50 years, with hundreds of children in and out of our home, I still don't know how we correct the damage done to these kids that are bounced from placement to placement. Love does not conquer all!

I think my eight-year-old may have put his finger on it when, after we both had become exasperated in the struggle to conquer his math homework, he looked over at me and said,

"Well, at my other school we learned it a different way than we are learning it here."

If each school teaches the same subjects in different ways, and each foster home has different rules and expectations, how can we expect an eight-year-old (or any age for that matter) to get past the nightmares and home-sickness enough to sort through the confusion that all these changes cause? Is it possible that *we* need to learn it a different way? I'm sure this chapter holds insights that will enlighten and encourage us all to keep on keeping on!

MARLENE, FOSTER PARENT OF 27 YEARS

Imagine, if you will, being taken away from your mother and your father, without any warning at all. Imagine being taken away from your siblings, your pets, your stuffed animals and toys. Imagine being taken away from your bedroom, house, yard, and neighborhood. Imagine, too, being taken from all of your relatives, friends, classmates, and everything you knew. In addition, after all of this, imagine if you were suddenly thrust into a strange house, with strangers, and informed that this was your new home and new family for the time being. How might you feel? For thousands upon thousands of children each year, this is not imagination, this is reality; and the reality is one that is full of questions, full of fears, and full of trauma.

As distressing as this may be for a child, even more traumatic may be that the removal from the child's birth home comes without any notification. These emergency removals often occur late in the evening, and with little to no warning for the children. As social workers remove a child from a home suddenly, most are unprepared. Foster children leave their home with a quick goodbye, leaving behind most of their belongings, with a few items of clothing and perhaps a prized possession hurriedly stuffed into a plastic bag. Before they know it, they are standing in front of you, strangers, people they have never met before. Against their will, they are in a strange home, their new home. With most children in foster care, it is a time of fear, a time of uncertainty, a time when even the bravest of children become scared. Indeed, foster children often have no control of this transition, no control of where they are placed, and no control of when they will go back to their birth family. It is this lack of control that often sends children in foster care spiraling into depression, various behavioral issues, and a world of anxiety.

Issues from anxiety can manifest themselves in a number of ways. Perhaps the one that foster children face the most is separation anxiety, an excessive concern that children struggle with concerning the separation from their home, family, and those they are attached to the most. Indeed, the more a child is moved, from home to home, from foster placement to another foster placement, or multiple displacements, the bigger the concern becomes. Those children who undergo multiple displacements often create walls to separate themselves in an attempt to not let others into their lives. In attempting to do so, many foster children end up lying to their foster families, as they try to keep their new family at a distance and at the same time give themselves a sense of personal control.

Children placed into foster care frequently suffer from mental health issues. A placement disruption may be so severe to the child that it feels as if their entire world is falling apart. For them, it is. Everything they know to be true in their world is now turned upside down. Their mother and father are no longer there to comfort them when they are troubled, or afraid. The family they lived with, grew up with, laughed with, and cried with is no longer there to take care of them. The bed they woke up in each morning is now different. For too many foster children, the school they went to, the teachers they learned from, and the friends they had formed relationships with, have also been taken from them. Instead, these children now live with a strange family, wake each morning in a different house, sit in an unfamiliar classroom, and are no longer surrounded by those who love and know them best. Children in foster care often struggle to best deal with and survive these traumatic events, as they struggle to adjust to a new home and new family. Not surprisingly, the losses in their life, along with the lack of a permanent home, often prevent these children from forming a secure and healthy attachment with a primary caregiver.

Sadly, the majority of foster children face the reality that most mental health problems are not being addressed as needed.

Furthermore, psychological and emotional issues that challenge foster children may even worsen and increase, rather than improve and decrease, while under placement in foster homes and care. Foster children, in many cases, do not receive adequate services in regard to mental health and developmental issues and will not likely do so in the near future, due to lack of government funding and lack of resources, as well as the simple matter that child welfare social workers are understaffed and overworked, in most states across the country.

Anxiety disorders

Issues from anxiety can manifest themselves in a number of ways. Perhaps the one that foster children face the most is separation anxiety, an excessive concern that children struggle with concerning the separation from their home, family, and those they are attached to the most. Indeed, the more a child is moved, the bigger the concern becomes.

Other anxiety disorders include *obsessive-compulsive disorder*, where a child repeats unwanted thoughts, actions, and/or behavior out of a feeling of need. *Panic disorders* find a child experiencing intense bouts of fear for reasons that may not be apparent. These attacks may be sudden and unexpected, as well as repetitive in their nature. Panic disorders also may coincide with strong physical symptoms, such as shortness of breath, dizziness, throbbing heartbeats, or chest pains. Another anxiety disorder that foster children may face is *social phobias*, or the fear of being embarrassed or facing the criticism of others.

Reactive Attachment Disorder

Reactive Attachment Disorder (R.A.D.) is a condition in which children have great difficulty in forming healthy attachments with others. Along with this, these children also struggle mightily with connecting with others on any type of social level. Children who are diagnosed with R.A.D. also find it very difficult to keep their emotions in control. Though often undiagnosed, many children in foster care suffer from R.A.D., a condition that their foster parents and social workers may not be familiar with.

Causes of Reactive Attachment Disorder

Every baby, indeed every child, needs to feel loved. Young children need to develop a feeling of trust with a loving adult, as well as develop a healthy loving bond between the caregiver and the child. If these simple emotional and physical needs are ignored, or instead met with emotional or physical abuse from the adult, attachment issues arise. Children who suffer from these conditions become distrustful of others, at the same time learning to avoid contact with others in a social setting, while at an early age. Though Reactive Attachment Disorder is rare, scientists have discovered that R.A.D. begins generally before a child reaches the age of five years, and most often during a child's infancy stage, or while a baby.

Children in foster care may develop R.A.D. for a number of reasons. To begin with, as the disorder is one that results in children having a difficult time socially interacting with others, those children in foster care who experience multiple displacements are more likely to develop R.A.D. Multiple displacement is the term used when a foster child moves from one foster home to another, then to another, on a frequent basis. Each move, each displacement, is another traumatic experience for the child. Indeed, each time a child is displaced, it is more difficult for the child to form a healthy, loving bond with another caregiver.

Sadly, a large number of children in foster care have suffered from extreme neglect from a biological family member or caregiver. These children have not had the opportunity to form the healthy attachment they sorely need as an infant. Other causes of Reactive Attachment Disorder stem from: physical, emotional, or sexual abuse at an early age; living in a home that is stricken with high levels of poverty; parental inexperience or abandonment; household alcohol or drug abuse; separation from a birth parent; prolonged periods of hospitalization; emotional instability, depression, or prolonged illness of a parent; or simple lack of daily engagement.

Signs and symptoms

As indicated earlier, R.A.D. can begin when a child is an infant. Thus, signs of the disorder can begin to show up in a child quite early in their life. Those babies who suffer from Reactive Attachment Disorder may appear to be withdrawn or sad. Not only do they often withdraw from others, they are also often unable to engage in any activity where another adult is attempting to pacify or soothe them, such as with stroking the child's head, or whispering to the baby with soothing words and a calming voice. Many babies with R.A.D. seldom, if ever, smile, despite the most persistent attempts from another. Along with this, lack of eye contact is another indication that the baby is suffering from the disorder, and the child will most likely not even have the inclination to follow someone with his or her eyes as the person walks across the room or passes in front of them. Another trait of those who suffer with the disorder is the failure to respond to interactive games with others, such as "peek-a-boo" and other games that engage small children.

As a child with Reactive Attachment Disorder grows older, the symptoms may grow more troublesome and difficult to manage. Anger issues may begin to develop, as the child might lash out in tantrums and/or uncontrolled rage, or act in a passive aggressive manner. While most with R.A.D. will endeavor to remain in control in an attempt to avoid a feeling of helplessness, often these children will instead act defiantly and disobediently, and will be quick to argue with others. Indeed, those who have problems with anger and control issues may be more likely to act in an aggressive manner toward their peers. Feelings of remorse or guilt for their negative actions and behavior are also often missing with those who are diagnosed with R.A.D.

While some children with R.A.D. may exhibit anger problems, others with the same disorder may be withdrawn, as they were in infancy. These children will seek to avoid interaction with others, including their peers, and act in an awkward and uncomfortable fashion while around others. Some children will strive to distance themselves from any type of physical contact with another, as they may perceive this interaction as a threat of some sort. Furthermore, these children will be more likely to seek

PLACEMENT DISRUPTIONS

out an affectionate relationship that is inappropriate with another, even those they do not know, yet display little or no affection toward their parents or caregivers.

Children with Reactive Attachment Disorder may display two different signs and patterns of their malady. *Inhibited behavior* is that in which the child will shun or discourage relationships and attachments with others. As noted previously, these are the children who are withdrawn or emotionally detached from others and from their surroundings. *Disinhibited behavior* occurs in those children who attempt to seek out attention from any and all who may be near, including strangers. These children will seek out comfort and attention from virtually anyone, yet at the same time will try to act very independently of others. Along with this, they will very likely refuse to ask for help or support from their peers. At times, children displaying disinhibited behavior will act much younger than their actual age, and also appear to be filled with high levels of anxiety.

Depression disorders

The loss of a family may result in a foster child spiraling into depression. These feelings of depression may intrude into all areas of a foster child's life, from their capability to act and function in the home to their school environment and the interaction with those their own age. Children who suffer from a depressive disorder may show strong and continuous signs of sadness. They may also have great difficulty in focusing on school work or life around them, and may instead concentrate on death or feelings of suicide. Loss of appetite or severe changes in eating habits may also be a result of a depressive disorder. Feelings of guilt over the placement may also overwhelm a foster child. Finally, a child who suffers from a depressive disorder may lack energy in day-to-day tasks, or may have difficulty sleeping.

Anger

Dealing with separation and loss is difficult for anybody. As an adult, you have had experience with this, and know who and

39

where to reach out to when in need of help. Foster children, though, generally do not know how to handle these feelings and emotions. Yet, these feelings must be released, in some fashion. One way of expressing these feelings of isolation is to lash out in anger and frustration to those around them. Though foster children do not necessarily blame the foster parent or the social worker, the feelings of frustration and loss are strong within them, and these carers may be the only ones they can release them to. Anger may also result in destruction of property or items within the foster home, as the child lashes out.

CHAPTER 3

School Academic Performance and Behavior

Early in my teaching career in Jasper County, about halfway through one year, when I was teaching all of the freshman classes at the old school, I got a new student, a shy young African-American girl. Nothing unusual about that, new students enter class on a fairly regular basis, but there was something different about this young lady. She was very shy, again nothing particularly unusual about this, most students are shy at first, but most begin to fit in after a few days. This young woman seemed to be especially withdrawn, as if she were protecting herself. I tend to allow my students plenty of time to adjust before I intervene. The problem here was that this young girl seemed to sink more and more deeply into her shell as the weeks went by. She almost never spoke, and when she did it was in a whisper. She did not mix with her peers or seek out friendships even when overtures from other students were made.

It was the middle of winter and I had caught a cold and had a cough I just could not get rid of. One day as I was reading a short story to the class I just couldn't continue because of my cough, and I asked the class to read silently. As I was walking up and down the aisle of the class monitoring their reading, and I passed the student's desk, she stretched out her hand and in it were two peppermints in their cellophane wrappers. She did not say a word, but made me this silent and sympathetic offering. I was taken back by this simple offering of kindness, thanked her and was able to resume reading. This simple unguarded gesture was a breakthrough, and from that day on she slowly and cautiously began to come out of her shell and join the class. She eventually became one of the better writers in the freshman class, and when she wrote about her personal experiences, she could rend your heart with her honest and remarkably mature prose.

It was not until much later, after this student and I began to slowly build a rapport with each other, and she learned to trust me and become a participating, contributing member of my class, that I learned that she was a foster child. I learned that she had been shunted from pillar to post among her extended family until she ended up in foster care, and that situation proved no better, because she bounced around in that system until she landed with a family in Monticello. I learned that this student had good reason to protect herself and to be wary of others and frightened of new situations. She was the daughter of a single mother who was barely out of childhood when this child was born. The mother had been the victim of abuse from maternal uncles, and this, in turn, had befallen the young woman I write about. Fortunately (if such a word can be applied here), for my student the abuse was limited to physical and emotional abuse—her mother had not been so lucky. While the mother had not been able to maintain a stable home for her daughter, she was determined that the same fate was not to befall her child, and it was the mother who first sought the foster placement.

The Monticello placement seemed to work for a while, but she was eventually reunited with her mother in Atlanta. I did learn that she graduated from high school, and I hope that she has prospered. I know I will never forget the impression that she made on me.

MICHAEL C., TEACHER OF 25 YEARS

School. For many children in foster care, it is the last place they want to be. For that foster child who has been taken from his or her family, from their home, from their friends, and all they know, and suddenly placed into a strange home late one evening, only to be forced to attend a strange school the following day, it is incredibly traumatic.

Let us examine Brandon, a 14-year-old foster child. Brandon was in ninth grade, and struggled with his academic studies. Placed into foster care due to parental neglect, abuse, and parental drug use, Brandon was never encouraged by his birth parents to succeed in school, and as a result, he was often behind in his classes. He was weak in English and math, and he often missed school, leading to issues of attendance. Brandon was placed in a home of a lawyer and a school secretary, two foster parents who valued education. He arrived at his foster home late one Tuesday evening, and was then enrolled into his new school the following morning by his social worker. As the school was unsure where to place him in classes, he was enrolled in college preparatory courses; courses which were too rigorous and academically challenging for him.

In his new English class, Brandon's teacher gave him a passage from *Romeo and Juliet* to read and analyze for homework. He was also given 25 math problems in his Algebra 1 course, a map to decipher in his Social Studies course, and a chapter to read and questions to answer in his Biology class. Lost in the school hallways a few times, Brandon was late to class twice, only to receive the curious stares from his new classmates, all strangers to him. Lunchtime posed other problems, as Brandon did not feel comfortable sitting with students he did not know. Upon discovering that Brandon was in foster care, many of the students asked Brandon if he was a "foster kid," creating further anxiety within him.

At one point in the afternoon, Brandon was bumped in the hall by another student between classes, his books flying across the hallway. Filled with feelings of doubt, confusion, anger, grief, loneliness, guilt, sadness, and fear, anxieties from being taken from his home and placed into care, along with the burdens of homework, a new school environment, and the stigma of being a "foster kid," Brandon lashed out at the student who had accidentally bumped into him. Yelling loudly, "Leave me alone, I just want to go home," Brandon abruptly pushed the other student against a nearby locker, thereby instigating a fight between the two. So, on Brandon's first day in his new school, the troubled teen's foster parents were called, informing them that he would be placed into the school's In School Suspension for the next three days. When Brandon returned home later that evening to his new foster home, the anxiety of the day, coupled with that from being placed into care, led to further emotional outbursts, as he informed his foster parents that he did not want to return to his new school the following day, or ever again for that matter.

As a result of the sudden and dramatic changes in their lives due to both the traumas suffered within their homes before placement and the trauma that placement into a foster home brings, many children in foster care have great difficulty in adjusting to school, both academically and behaviorally. These challenges include the academic, social, and emotional turmoil caused by placement disruptions and adjustment to a new school environment (Vericker, Kuehn, and Capps 2007). Grief, anxiety, loss, confusion, anger, sadness, loneliness, and low self-worth are some of the emotions that foster teens may experience when encountering placement disruption (Simms, Dubowitz, and Szilagyi 2000). As Bowlby's theory of attachment would suggest (see Bowlby 1982), many children might have a difficult time forming relationships with students and teachers because of continuous placement disruptions in their lives. As foster children are only a small percentage of the total makeup of students in a classroom setting, often less than 1 percent (Jackson and Sachdev 2001), this may explain why there has not been much research interest in the foster care program as it relates to those foster children who are enrolled in public schools.

Foster children, in general, tend to perform below average in regard to both academic performance and positive behavior compared with those students who come from traditional homes as well as children from economically disadvantaged homes (Altshuler 1997; Ayasse 1995; Finkelstein *et al.* 2000). Zima *et al.* (2000) found that 69 percent of children under foster care supervision experience problems in behavior while enrolled in public schools. These behavioral problems may be indicated by feelings of aggressiveness, which result in aggressive behavior toward others (Ayasse 1995). It has been found that children who are angry and frustrated are more prone to experience conduct problems (Deater-Deckard, Petrill, and Thompson 2007). Foster children may also experience feelings of low self-esteem, delinquency, and disruptive behavior (Ayasse 1995). They tend to be demanding and lack maturity as they seek the attention of those around them.

For many foster children, school is a constant reminder that they are, indeed, foster children without a true home. Their peers are living with biological family members while they are not. This can be a difficult reality for them, and can be manifested in several ways, such as displaying aggressive behavior, disruptive behavior, defiance, and low self-esteem (Zima *et al.* 2000). Some foster children simply withdraw and become antisocial, in an attempt to escape the current environment into which they have been thrust (Stein *et al.* 1996). For many foster children, violent behavior becomes the norm, as they not only act out in a negative and disruptive fashion in the school, but also in their foster home. This can prompt another move to another foster home and another school (Ayasse 1995).

As a result of this behavior, foster children often face greater risks of suspension from school, affecting their academic standing. They may repeat a grade level, or are simply placed in classes that are not appropriate to their age level (Benedict, Zuravin, and Stallings 1996; Berrick, Barth, and Needell 1994; Sawyer and Dubowitz 1994; Smucket and Kauffman 1996; Zetlin, Weinberg, and Shea 2006). Mason *et al.* (2004), using data from the Seattle Social Development Program, found in their study of 800 school-aged children in the Seattle, Washington, area that those children who suffer from depression have a much higher rate of behavior disorders, including violent behavior, which often results in school suspension.

Children in care often move from school to school. The following are several examples provided by a social worker from the state of Georgia:

- A 13-year-old boy was enrolled in the school for three days, with no records or transcripts accompanying him from a previous school before moving to another county.

- A 14-year-old girl was enrolled in the school for 27 days, also with no transcripts or records before she, too, was placed in another county.

- A 17-year-old girl was placed in a foster home for 120 of the 180 calendar school days, before she was placed in a group home in a nearby city and transferred schools. The records and transcripts of this foster teen did follow her, though it took a period of three months to do so. As a result, the school had difficulty placing her in the appropriate courses and was also unable to address any issues in regard to learning disabilities.

◆ A 14-year-old girl was enrolled in the school for a year and a half before being adopted by family members outside the state of Georgia, precipitating yet another move for the teenager.

◆ Another foster child was in need of special tutoring services that the county's school system could not deliver. As a result, the student had to be driven to a city further away in a nearby county, not only draining a great deal of time, but also at a great expense to the county's Department of Family and Children Services.

New placements may translate to frustration and behavior disorders, due to the lack of stability in the foster child's life, as he or she endeavors to create new relationships on a continuous basis (Emerson and Lovitt 2003). Foster children often express these behavior problems because of the large amounts of school time missed with court appearances, doctors' appointments, or simply from multiple placements (Davey and Pithouse 2008; Parrish *et al.* 2001). High levels of absenteeism frequently lead to grade retention, which leads to frustration and behavioral problems (Parrish *et al.* 2001). Those children who experience multiple placements may face the dilemma of not obtaining the special needs in regard to specific services to assist them with learning disabilities/impairments, as schools often do not have the time necessary to implement appropriate testing (Weinberg, Weinberg, *et al.* 1997).

An Australian study of children enrolled in five primary schools found that foster children wished to form strong, meaningful relationships with their teachers, but this was impossible if the child encounters multiple placements in multiple schools, resulting in frustration and possible behavior disorders (Howard and Johnson 2000). The authors of this study determined this through a three-year study using an interview process with 125 students aged 9–12 and 25 teachers in an economically depressed area of South Australia. Yet, not only is a foster child's school performance affected by behavior disorders, but problems with emotional, mental, and health-related issues also affect school performance (Ayasse 1995). Many children who are removed from their homes and placed into foster care enter the child welfare system with chronic health, developmental, and even psychiatric disorders, because of neglect and abuse they faced while in their birth homes. Add to this the emotional distress and suffering that occurs when the children are separated, or removed, from their birth parents (Simms *et al.* 2000).

Using computerized claims in regard to Medicaid insurance, dosReis *et al.* (2001) were able to establish a population-based prevalence estimate of children with mental disorders. This one-year cross-sectional analysis of youth mental health services study using 15,507 foster children found that 57 percent of these children had some type of mental disorder. Those foster children who were taken from homes due to neglect repeatedly suffer from a number of developmental delays. These include poor language and vocabulary development, thus impairing communication skills. Antisocial behavior, and even poor brain development, may result from neglect (American Academy of Pediatrics 2000). Indeed, a survey study by Stahmer *et al.* (2005) of 2813 children found this to be true, and asserted that those children referred to child welfare agencies, such as the Department of Family and Children (DFCS), have severe mental developmental problems.

Studies have also determined that there are high levels of mental health problems with children under foster care, and that these mental health problems are not being addressed as needed (Clausen *et al.* 1998; Horwitz, Owens, and Simms 2000). Furthermore, psychological and emotional issues that challenge foster children may even worsen and increase, rather than improve and decrease, while under placement in foster homes and care (Simms *et al.* 2000). Foster children, in many cases, do not receive adequate services in regard to mental health and developmental issues and will not likely do so in the near future (Pecora *et al.* 2009).

One study found that as many as 66 percent of children placed under foster care supervision suffer from at least one learning-based developmental delay (Leslie *et al.* 2002). Another study went even further, and maintained that over 80 percent of foster children suffered from behavioral issues (Halfon, Mendonca, and Berkowitz 1995). As many foster children encounter multiple displacements, it is highly likely that these students will receive neither the remediation nor the necessary services they require in regard to developmental delays (Stock and Fisher 2006).

As indicated previously, foster children frequently suffer from language delay. Multiple studies have indicated that language developmental delays range from 35 percent to 73 percent of all children in foster care (Amster, Greis, and Silver 1997; George *et al.* 1992; Halfon *et al.* 1995; Hochstadt *et al.* 1987; Simms 1989; Stahmer *et al.* 2005). Math and reading skills also appear to be weak within the ranks of foster children, with 23 percent of this population suffering from severe delays in both reading and math (Zima *et al.* 2000).

Indeed, foster children are at greater risk of struggling in school, both academically and socially, than those children who come from traditional homes, resulting in generally lower standardized test scores and poorer grades, as well as behavioral problems often culminating in suspension from the school (Weinberg, Zetlin, *et al.* 2009). Thirty percent of children in the custody of child welfare agencies exhibit the need for special education services (Webb *et al.* 2007). This is in comparison to the 9.16 percent of the total amount of all students who require these services in public schools (U.S. Department of Education 2009). In addition, students in foster care exhibit an array of academic difficulties, including cognitive abilities that are weaker than those of traditional students (Althshuler 1997). Federal and state funding to assist in this problem is lacking (Weinberg, Zetlin, *et al.* 2009).

The placement of a foster child into a new foster home not only brings difficulties within the child's school performance, but also into the lives of those within the foster home. Foster parents are assigned the task of ensuring the foster child's wellbeing and needs, such as food, clothing, and shelter. This task is expected of the foster parents in a full-time capacity, both night and day, as the foster child comes to live within the home in a sense of permanency, as this placement may last for many months, to multiple years.

A recent study (AFCARS 2009, pp.1–2) found the following time frames in the foster care system:

* 5 percent of foster children remained in foster care for less than 1 month.

* 37 percent of foster children remained in foster care for 1 to 11 months.

* 23 percent of foster children remained in foster care for 12 to 23 months.

* 12 percent of foster children remained in foster care for 24 to 35 months.

* 9 percent of foster children remained in foster care for 36 to 59 months.

* 14 percent of foster children remained in foster care for 5 or more years.

Some foster children are not granted visitation with their birth families because of incarceration of the birth parents; however, most foster children are granted visitation rights. These visitations most often occur at the office of the social worker, or within the home of the foster parents (Davis *et al.* 1996). However, neither of these environments is a model one, as the social worker's office may increase the frustrations associated with the situation, increasing the tension felt by all, while visitation within the foster parents' home may also be met with tension, as foster parents and the birth parents all experience feelings of anxiety over a sense of loyalty and duty in regard to the child's welfare (McVey and Mullis 2004). Results from a study by Cantos, Gries, and Slis (1997) indicated that children who had irregular visits with birth parents tended to exhibit increased levels of misbehavior and deviance compared with those foster children who attended regular intervals of visitations.

As indicated earlier, school performance may suffer due to placement disruptions. Althshuler (1987) demonstrated that many foster children suffer from weaker cognitive skills, thus leading to poorer academic performances in the classroom. As a result, many foster children are retained, thus repeating the same grade a second time, and are also placed in classes below their age groups (Benedict *et al.* 1996; Berrick *et al.* 1994; Canning 1974; Harden 2004; Mata 2009; Sawyer and Dubowitz 1994; Smucket and Kauffman 1996). This may also be due to the increased levels of absenteeism that foster children face while under foster care supervision (Parrish *et al.* 2001). Parrish *et al.* (2001) found in their study of California children's group homes that the increased absenteeism in foster children was due to displacement disorders, as well as lack of support or motivation by others in their lives. As foster children often experience multiple placement disruptions, schools often do not have the appropriate amount of time to test the child for possible learning disabilities, thus prolonging the lack of possible assistance in this area for the child (Weinberg, Weinberg, *et al.* 1997; Weinberg, Zetlin, *et al.* 2003).

CHAPTER 4

Aging Out of the System

As I think back on my own life experiences as a foster child, it really is some kind of miracle I made it to my high school graduation. I recall having been burdened by the struggles of being abused, a runaway, a drop-out, attempting suicide, moving from the north to the south three times, and lacking all family love, guidance, and support. Yet, somehow, I graduated from high school. Today, I realize that the demands on all children to excel in academia, along with increased expectations for advanced performance in other areas of their lives, is quite daunting. The guidance parents provide is akin to some kind of master plan ensuring their children have a good start in life; but for people like me, the foster child, it's a completely different road to travel.

On average, foster children are not prepared to participate in AP or Honors classes nor are extra-curricular activities readily available to them. The opportunities to volunteer that are required for some colleges and personal growth are nil, there is minimal and bleak parental guidance, if any at all, and part-time work is not usually accessible to them, so there goes their foundational experience and resume-building. Additionally, there isn't really much serious talk, if any, in the home of which college they plan to attend or how to begin that journey because more often than not there aren't any invested parents available to assist in the development of such a plan. Foster children are doing all they can to just survive the turbulence of today while dealing with the shadows of their past, the traumatic memories of their parents, and this moment of depression, chaos, and sometimes dark thoughts of suicide.

Before delving into the challenges they face upon emancipation, let's first look at what precipitates their challenges. First and of great importance is to know at what age did they enter the foster care system, how many times did they move, and how inconsistent has their education been? I wish I could address one of these concerns without the other two but that would be unfair to the foster child because they all directly affect the challenges these children face as they approach emancipation.

The age at which they enter foster care directly affects to what extent they are psychologically affected. This affects their sense-of-identity and their self-esteem, both crucial for healthy development. For how long have they heard the stigma-based introduction of "This is my foster child"? On how many holidays have they felt like the odd ball in the room? For how long has this psychological damage been cemented into their psyche? The number of times they've moved from foster home to foster home and school to school will directly affect their sense-of-belonging in any micro- or macro-system. Each time a child moves, they suffer social, educational, and psychological maladies from instability. Their lack of self-worth amplifies their challenge to socially acclimate. "To feel or not to feel accepted and understood by others" can be the difference between resiliency and pathology.

The second tier of challenges foster youth face as they approach emancipation is "Do they have a trustworthy and consistent support system?" This element is needed for all youth transitioning different life stages but the dichotomy for foster children is in their suffering of exasperated burdens from not only lacking a solid family to provide guidance and emotional support, but also to be able to have long-term trusted relationships with people who have their best interest at heart. Who are we as a species if we do not have long-term support from trusted relationships? All of these negative elements are exponentially multiplied in their future if they do not graduate high school. I often say, "Leaving foster care without a high school diploma is like trying to climb a ladder that doesn't have any steps." It's nearly impossible to progress. If a foster child does not have the proper family support and does not have a high school diploma, how can they succeed? The outlook is grim, thus, our nation currently suffers from tens of thousands of homeless, unemployed, and/or incarcerated foster care alumni because as it is, nearly half leave foster care without having graduated.

A high school diploma is their primary asset which provides for an even playing field from which they can progress. Despite their emotional and financial burdens, a high school diploma opens the gates for independent living, future opportunities, increased self-esteem, and enrichment of life's possibilities.

As they become more aware of the opportunities available to them, their high school diploma will provide the means of entry to excel; but without a diploma, their mountainous deficits magnify the probability that they will perish.

CAPRI C., FOSTER CHILD ALUMNA

Being placed in a foster home is bad enough for a child. Sadly, for far too many foster children, leaving the foster care system is even more traumatic. As a foster child reaches the age of eighteen in most states, and 21 years in other states, the child "ages out" of the foster system, and begins the transition into "the real world."

Eighteen years old is a difficult time for any teenager. Certainly for many teens, it is a time of independence, freedom, and change; at least it is in the eyes of many when they reach that magic age. It is a time of moving out of a home, finding a job, joining the military, and going off to college. Typically, children from traditional homes have parents who are able to guide them through these changes, providing help and advice as these 18-year-olds determine the next stage in their lives. Along with this, most young adults are still able to rely on their parents not only for good advice, but also for help financially. In truth, we do not expect our teens to experience adulthood overnight, nor do we abandon them and leave them to fend for themselves. For many teens from traditional homes who are turning 18 years of age, their parents, family members, and adult friends are still there for them; still there to provide help, information, and resources. Indeed, many of these teens are able to return home if times and circumstances should become too difficult for them.

For most young adults leaving home for the first time, they have someone to rely on when facing challenges, difficulties, and trials. In many cases, this adult is a loving parent, one who has raised the child since birth, cared for the child during times of sickness, helped the child with school work, and provided for the child throughout their life. Other children may have been raised and cared for by grandparents, relatives, or adoptive parents. Later, after leaving the home for college, military, career, or other post-high school possibilities, these children have an adult to call upon when they are faced with challenges or need help. They can return home for holidays, or may simply receive a card or phone call from the adult on a birthday. Whether the problems are financial, emotional, school oriented, or simply a flat tire that needs to be fixed, most young adults can pick up a phone and call an adult who is quick to help. These adults will be there for the young adults.

Foster children, though, do not have these resources, these lifelines so to speak, to help out as they try to ease into their own lives of independence. If the teen should become sick, there is no one to take care of them, no one to make them a bowl of hot soup. On their birthday, there is no one who will send them a birthday card, or sing "Happy Birthday" to them. If their car should break down, there is no one to help them get it fixed, or even help change a flat tire. On holidays, there is no one who is inviting the young adult over to celebrate as a family. If the teen should graduate from high school, sadly there often is no one sitting in attendance at the graduation ceremony, supporting and encouraging them. For those former foster youth who do make it to college, there is no home to return to for the vacations. Simply put, there is no family for this young adult; no one to help, no one to act as a mentor, no one to turn to in an emergency, and no one to give advice when it may be needed the most.

Each year, between 20,000 and 25,000 foster children age out of the system and attempt to begin life on their own. Along with this, another 5200 youth in foster care run away before reaching the age of 18 (Swift 2007). For many foster children, foster care is a temporary service before returning home to a parent, moving in with a biological family member, or even beginning a new life in an adopted home. Yet, for thousands who do not find reunification with family, reaching 18 years of age can be a tremendously frightening experience. For others, 21 is the age where they may find themselves no longer part of the foster care system, depending upon the state the foster children reside in. Tragically, most state-sponsored policies that have services which support foster children while in care cease when the child turns 18, or becomes an adult. As a result, these youth face challenges and obstacles when simply trying to meet their most basic needs. Without the help from loving parents, supportive adults, or even the government, many former foster youth often struggle while merely trying to survive. Indeed, without a high school diploma, these struggles and challenges become even more difficult.

Homelessness

Former foster youth have a very difficult time when trying to maintain stable housing. Imagine for yourself trying to pay for housing, food, utilities, and all that corresponds with living on your own, while 18 years of age, with no help from anyone else. While there are those young adults who are able to accomplish this successfully, it is both uncommon and rather difficult.

Foster youth who age out of care often leave the foster system without the necessary skills, experiences, or knowledge they need in order to best adjust to society. Without a family to turn to once they age out, many foster children find themselves in difficult times and situations. These young adults, who are involuntarily separated from their foster families through the intervention of the government, face higher rates of homelessness as most have no options for future housing. As a result of these obstacles and challenges, most foster children who age out of the system find themselves at risk in several ways. To begin with, when foster children leave the foster care system, they often have no place to call home. Over half of all youth who age out of the system end up being homeless at one point at least once in their young lives. As they struggle with financial problems, finding a safe and stable place to call home is often hard. Too many foster children are forced to turn to the streets for a time. If they are fortunate, they may end up in a homeless shelter, but this is often not the case.

Recently, the Midwest Study, a large-scale longitudinal study by Chapin Hall, invited former foster youth to take part in a study. The Midwest Study concluded that former foster youth were twice as likely as peers their same age to be unable to pay for their mortgage or rent (Courtney and Dworsky 2005). Along with this, the state of Massachusetts found that 25 percent of homeless young adults aged 18–24 were former foster care youth (Massachusetts Society for Prevention for Cruelty to Children 2005). In the state of California, an astonishing 65 percent of former foster youth who age out were without secured housing (California Department of Social Services 2002).

For some former foster youth, housing with kinship carers may be an option. Kinship care is the practice of placing youths in the home of extended relatives and family members, such as grandparents, aunts and uncles, and others related to the youth. Though housing with kinship carers may provide more stability, research does indicate that these former foster youths often live in poverty "with caregivers who are elderly, single, or poorly educated" (Goelitz 2007). Furthermore, many kinship carers are not entitled to the same financial support systems and resources that licensed foster parents are. Thus, these carers, and the youths, do not have the same access to medical, financial, and educational services and resources that youth in foster care have (Goelitz 2007).

Unemployment

Unemployment is higher in former foster children, and many struggle financially. This may be due to the fact that roughly 50 percent of those foster youth who age out do not complete high school. They are more than twice as likely not to have a high school diploma than others their own age, and only six percent graduate from a two or four year college with a degree (AFCARS 2009). Clearly, as many foster children do not graduate from high school, they find it difficult to obtain a job that will be able to provide for them financially. Added to this, most simply do not have the skills, training, or tools necessary for procuring a stable job, or even a job at all.

One study concluded that only 40 percent of 19-year-old former foster teens had a job of some sort. Of these, 90 percent earned less than ten thousand dollars during the year. Of those foster teens who had a job, 55 percent had been fired from their job at least once after leaving care (Courtney and Dworsky 2005). Yet another troubling study concluded that 24 percent of former foster youth supported themselves financially by selling drugs, while 11 percent did so through means of prostitution (Eyster and Oldmixon 2007).

Poverty

As so many former foster youth struggle with lack of employment, a lack of education or high school diploma, as well as the issue of homelessness, it should be no surprise that a large number also face poverty, or economic instability.

According to the findings in the Midwest Study, only 46 percent of former foster youth had a savings or checking bank account opened in their name, as opposed to 82 percent of their peers. Along with this, those foster teens that aged out of the system are twice as likely not to have enough money needed in order to pay for rent. Roughly 25 percent of males and over 50 percent of females receive government assistance in one form or another, including food stamps and public housing or rental assistance. Finally, the study also concluded that over half of those foster teens who aged out experience at least one of the following: disconnected electrical, gas, or phone services; eviction; homelessness; lack of food; or lack of money to pay for housing and/or food (Courtney and Dworsky 2005).

Criminal activity

It comes as no surprise that many former foster youth end up in some sort of incarceration. Many foster children who age out also turn to drugs and even crime, thus resulting in jail sentences. Indeed, the percentage of foster youth who aged out and spent some time in jail is 41 percent (Courtney and Heuring 2005). Another disturbing number comes from the state of California where the number of former foster youth who have spent time in jail is a staggering statistic at well over 70 percent (Select Committee Hearing of the California Legislature 2006). Furthermore, one half of male former foster youth in California with prison records had been sentenced for committing violent or serious crimes (Needell *et al.* 2002). Still another study concluded that the more time youths were placed under foster care supervision, the more likely they were to encounter violence while in a romantic relationship with another (Reilly 2003). Sadly, 13 percent of females who spent time in foster care reported to have been sexually assaulted and/or raped within twelve to eighteen months after leaving the foster care system (Courtney and Heuring 2005).

Independent living skills

For many children who age out of the foster care system, simple independent living skills are lacking. These basic, yet necessary, skills that require them to live independently of others in a successful and healthy fashion very often are not taught to them; whether from parental figures and adults, or while in school. Skills such as cooking meals, driving a car, finding housing, keeping appointments, managing a bank account, shopping for groceries and household items, and taking public transportation are missing in many children who age out (Wolanin 2005). Without the proper knowledge of managing a bank account, financial problems will likely arise. Lack of transportation knowledge will hinder the young adult from obtaining or holding a steady job. For those foster youth who age out and do not have a supportive parental figure in their life, it may be quite difficult, or even impossible, for them to sign proper paperwork regarding housing as well as information about credit history when trying to obtain financial loans (Gilpatrick 2007).

Healthcare and mental health

Proper healthcare also remains a problem for former foster children. While under the care of a child welfare system, foster children do in fact receive free healthcare through Medicaid. Medical treatment and essential medicine are the right of each foster child while under care. Yet, when a child ages out, this healthcare is no longer provided, leaving many without any type of insurance or care, with one study reporting the percentage of foster youth without health insurance at 55 percent (Reilly 2003). Along with this, access to mental health and additional support organizations is also difficult to come by, with only 25 percent on Medicaid (Reilly 2003). Many of these former foster youth also suffer from health problems related to maternal substance abuse, parental neglect, physical abuse, and sexual abuse (Gerber and Dicker 2006).

Accordingly, countless former foster children have untreated mental health needs (Courtney and Heuring 2005). Recent studies have found that adults who have spent time in foster care suffer from the ravages of post-traumatic stress disorder (Plotkin 2005). So widespread is this amongst former foster children that it is double the rate of those US combat veterans who suffer from it (Plotkin 2005). Indeed, many youth who leave foster care suffer from a number of mental health disorders, including depression, high anxiety levels, and mental illnesses, with one study finding the percentage to be as high as 91 percent (McMillen *et al.* 2004). Along with this, large numbers of these young adults face the trials of not having proper healthcare and insurance, as they lose the coverage that was provided for them while in care. Many simply do not have someone to care for them when they fall sick or face medical emergencies.

Pregnancies

Aged-out female foster youth also have higher pregnancy rates than females their own age from traditional homes, with one study concluding that the number is nearly three times as many (Shaw *et al.* 2010). Furthermore, nearly 50 percent of young women were pregnant inside of a year to eighteen months after leaving the foster care system (Sullivan 2009).

Pregnancy levels at an early age are a greater risk among those females who have spent time in foster care, and many young men who age out of the system unexpectedly find themselves fathers and are unable to properly provide for the child (Courtney and Heuring 2005). Not surprisingly, former foster youth are more likely to raise children out of wedlock than their peers, with less than one third of these former foster mothers in a married relationship (Courtney and Heuring 2005).

Tragically, for many former foster youth, the cycle of deprivation, with these challenges, continues from one generation to the next, as 19 percent of parents who were former foster children reported having their own children removed from their home and placed into the supervision of foster care (Courtney and Heuring 2005).

Certainly, it is a bleak future that most foster children face as they age out of a system; a system that may have failed them with the resources, training, and support they sorely need in order to be a success, or even a positive contribution to society. Without a proper education, and a high school diploma, this future becomes even more grim, as they struggle mightily to make it in a world that has already shown them much pain, trauma, grief, and sorrow.

CHAPTER 5

Why Teachers, Social Workers, and Foster Parents Struggle

Life in foster care can be particularly challenging and disruptive for kids and teens, emotionally and developmentally. The book *The Connected Child* (Purvis, Cross, and Sunshine 2007) articulates well that perhaps our greatest challenge as foster parents, teachers, and social workers is "it takes time to glimpse the full depth of the harm their child may have endured in his or her 'former' life, and how it connects to the challenges he or she faces today. Children can bring with them: abandonment, loss, and grief issues; cognitive impairments; fear, anger, post-traumatic stress; shame, anxiety, and depression. These impairments can be hard to recognize so adults can be less likely to be compassionate and helpful about the challenges these kids face."

The teens we see in our ministry have needs and dreams like any other kids—with the exception of having suffered trauma and loss through no fault of their own. These are kids who have experienced severe abuse and/or neglect due to crises of parenting such as poverty, substance abuse, incarceration, mental illness, and homelessness.

At the ministry of Rick Rack, in the state of Michigan, we see recurring challenges in schools that teens face. We see two common themes from these challenges: teens that lack support and teens that have strong community connections.

In ministry we witness foster teens' lack of educational opportunities caused by instability in their personal life. Most who are in high school bounce from group homes to foster homes to shelters, resulting in high numbers of placement changes and broken relationships. What we know through our time with each teen is that most teens cannot handle both the stress of their private life and the strictness of their academic courses. On the other hand, they are very aware that a diploma is the dream that could change futures. With the enormous education gap and instability they face, they tend to give up on traditional schooling and settle for alternative schools or simply drop out.

Permanent, supportive relationships and connections are critical to young adults' wellbeing, especially those in foster care that have many placement changes and need much guidance. Teens who maintain relationships with former foster families and their community connections are happier and more stable. We see this again and again in our ministry. Once they know they have the commitment of each relationship they do better in school, form healthy relationships, and even talk with hope about their futures. They feel safe when they are heard and when parents, teachers, and social workers advocate for their needs and helping to close the gap in their education.

Rachel was 16 when we met her through our clothed-in-love program. The first time she came to us she was one of the saddest-looking girls we knew. Her story is another story of betrayal. Not by only one parent, but both. Rachel had a dark secret that crushed her spirit and she finally shared it with her mother. She had been dealing with her father who was molesting her. The heartbreak is that her mother called her a liar and kicked her out of the home she knew. She was then placed in her aunt's home in a nearby city. Her aunt became her surrogate mother and advocate. She advocated for Rachel, to the school, social worker, and therapist. In addition, Rachel joined the Michigan Youth Opportunity Initiative group, an outreach group for teens aging out of the foster care system. Her home life became stable and her grades began to improve. While she was healing in her new environment she began 4-H youth development training, received her driver's license, started working at a candy shop, and graduated from high school. Rachel is still healing but is happier because of the support she has received from her aunt, Michigan Youth Opportunities Initiative group, and Rick Rack Ministry. She continues to dream of one day going to college. I hope you do, Rachel.

CASANDRA C., RICK RACK MINISTRY FOUNDER

Today's society is a busy one. It seems that all working adults are busy. Perhaps busy is not the correct word. Perhaps a better word might be overwhelmed. As more and more organizations face the stark reality of budget cuts and funding issues, for many government employees, as well as those in the private workforce, there do not seem to be enough hours in the day to accomplish all the needs to be attended to. Indeed, foster parents, social workers, and teachers all face the same dilemma: they are under-resourced, underpaid, overworked, and overwhelmed.

A successful working relationship and collaboration may not exist between public schools, foster parents, birth parents, and child welfare agencies. Consequently, foster children do not receive the services they require in order to be successful. Yet, education is considered crucially important for many foster children in regard to the quality of life they wish to have in their adult life. Sadly, many students in foster care are not getting the necessary support they need from their foster parents, their social workers, and school employees. Without this support, the student is almost destined to fail in academic studies, and struggle with behavioral issues.

In spite of this, all three sets of adult support groups grapple with figuring out how to best help these troubled children, all to the detriment of the child in need. School counselors, in general, have been ineffective in meeting the needs of those students who are foster children, yet the need is growing for these school employees to do so, as the population of foster children continues to escalate. Some social workers have, in the past, also neglected the school life of foster children, and ignored educational policies and procedures. Foster parents also play a role in this. In truth, there are a number of reasons why these caregivers, social workers, and educators find it difficult to help children in foster care.

Teachers

In many schools in the early part of the twenty-first century, funding cuts and budget issues have resulted in a most difficult workplace for today's educators. Today's teachers are no longer responsible for only teaching the child. Teachers today have so many more roles and responsibilities placed upon their shoulders; roles and responsibilities that almost overshadow their classroom instructional time.

Gone are the days when a student would have their mother kiss them on the cheek as they merrily left to walk to school, handing an apple to their teacher right before they sat behind their desk, with a smile on their face, eager to learn. Gone are those days when all the teacher had to do was teach the child reading, writing, and arithmetic. Today's teachers wear many different hats, and have many more duties to perform, as today's school systems have more expectations from their teachers.

To begin with, today's educators have more testing that they are responsible for. Not only do students have the traditional test at the end of each chapter or unit, but also teachers are now responsible for preparing their students for local, state, and federal testing. These tests may consist of pre-tests and post-tests for each unit studied, benchmark tests, standardized tests, end-of-course tests, final exams, and other tests that the school or course might require. This large amount of testing is not only stressful to both students and teachers, but also requires a great deal of planning on the part of the teacher. To make this even more difficult, many school districts hold their teachers accountable for their students' test scores, results, and grades, basing job performance assessment upon test results. Consequently, the greater amount of testing and the accountability adds further stress and pressure to educators.

Along with testing, schools also demand more learning-based evidence. Teachers are expected to have more graded tasks from their students, showing evidence that learning is taking place within their classrooms. Homework assignments, classroom projects, reports, essays, quizzes, and other daily graded tasks are now part of today's classroom expectations. With more tests and more learning-based evidence projects comes more grading from teachers. Indeed, it is quite common for teachers to not only spend many additional hours in their classroom after school each day, grading student work, but also to take home folders and bags full of paperwork each evening and weekend, spending large amounts of personal and family time attending to all the grading that is required so as not to fall behind. The task of grading is one that can quickly turn into an avalanche, inundating a teacher with the heavy workload.

Educators also have to plan for more standardized courses and classes. With more testing and grading comes more teaching. The need for preparation for classroom instruction and learning has increased substantially through the years. Couple this with the various meetings that are required of teachers, both throughout the school day as well as after school, for which teachers today often have to deal with supplementary paperwork. Additionally, the everyday workload of the twenty-first century educator includes paperwork regarding parental contact, student progress, student behavioral and conduct reports, and other learning and behavioral-based reports. Moreover, many school principals require that their teachers turn in weekly lesson plans ahead of time, thus calling for teachers to plan even further in advance. Finally, with added tasks such as lunch room, bus ramp, hall monitoring duties, after-school sports and school clubs/organizations, and dances, as well as the responsibility of keeping up with the latest trends in education, changes in classroom standards, and advances in technology, it is no wonder that teachers can become overwhelmed with all that is required of them. Indeed, the many additional responsibilities and expectations leave little time to actually teach.

As society does not truly understand nor appreciate what children in foster care go through each day, nor the foster care system in general, it is not surprising that today's teachers do not, either. While many teachers may have some knowledge about foster care, it is doubtful that there is full understanding. Indeed, it is likely that many teachers are not entirely aware of why a child might be placed into care, what the child goes through on a daily basis emotionally, how foster parenting works, and how the foster care system works, as a whole.

In truth, it is almost impossible in today's educational climate for a teacher to truly help a student in foster care. To start with, teachers are not trained about foster children and the foster care system. While foster parents undergo rigorous and extensive training before taking a child into their homes, training that helps to prepare them for the many emotional, physical, and mental challenges that often accompany children in care, teachers and educators do not have any training in this field. There are many challenges that children in foster care experience, due to the unique traumas they have faced; traumas that require specific training and understanding in order to best meet the needs of these troubled children. Typically, teachers are not trained in this area, through no fault of their own. Along with this, there is very little literature on foster children and schools that is available, making it even more difficult for those teachers and school employees who wish to learn more on the matter.

Furthermore, it is quite likely that teachers do not know that there is a foster child in their classroom, as there are numerous and specific privacy laws in place in regard to student information. Consider the words from one high school teacher from the state of Georgia, USA:

> Quite frankly, I didn't know much about foster care, or about foster children. I always thought that foster children were those children who were placed into another home because of problems of discipline, or drugs, or some other issue that either they or their parents were responsible for. That's it. I never gave it another thought. One year, the school counselor came to me and told me that one of my students' foster parents wanted to have a conference with me. I was very surprised, as I didn't know that I had a foster child in my class. The student was quiet and withdrawn, and I simply thought she was shy. I found out, later, that she had been sexually abused many times by her stepfather. I wish I had known. I wish I had known that she was a foster child. I wish I had known that she was facing her own traumas. I would have reached out to her more, and been more understanding when it came to her homework, and classroom participation. I think that all teachers should know if they have a foster child who is a student in their classroom, as I believe that it will help all involved.

JOSHUA K., MATH TEACHER

Like Joshua K., many teachers do not know that there are foster children sitting in their classrooms. As a result, these students can quickly "fall through the cracks" and not receive the resources, understanding, and simple compassion from the school teacher that they may sorely need. Other teachers may have the belief that foster children come and go within their classrooms and school so quickly and rapidly, as they are placed from home to home, that it may not be necessary to build a relationship with the student or, for that matter, spend the effort getting the student "caught up with the rest of the class" in regard to school content and learning:

> Well, I've only had a few [foster teens] in my classes and the biggest problem with them is that they tend not to stay, so it's hard to form a relationship because they're here one day then gone the next...you don't have time to get to form a relationship.

DEGARMO 2011

As indicated earlier in Chapters 1 and 3, often children in foster care are placed into schools without transcripts and/or school records. When a foster child is enrolled in a school without past transcripts from a previous school(s), school officials have the complicated task of placing the child into appropriate classes; classes that they have not already taken, are suitable for their learning ability, and are appropriate for them, in general. For the classroom teacher who has a student who is without transcripts or records, this can be most challenging, and even frustrating. The information found in these transcripts and school records is essential to better understand a student's needs, in regard to both behavior and academic studies. When a student is placed into a classroom without this information, often teachers will have difficulty meeting the individual's academic needs, as well as being prepared for any behavioral issues that the child may face:

> For the teachers to know they're foster kids and to have a little information into their background, whether there are any abuse issues or etc. [sic] that could cause learning disabilities for a lack of a better word...knowing the background on them. I like to know a little about their home life. It helps me adapt to teaching them.

DEGARMO 2011

As noted earlier, foster children face their own set of unique traumas and challenges, which may result in behavior disorders while in school. If a foster child should react or behave in a way during the school day that results in him or her having to be disciplined by a teacher or school administrator, the information contained on school records is quite helpful in better understanding the nature of the child's behavior, and how to best address it; thus better meeting the foster child's needs during the time of trauma that comes along with multiple displacement, or moving from home to home and school to school. School counselors, also, frequently lack a foster child's background information that is so essential. Without this information, the school counselor is hindered greatly when attempting to understand the child and his needs.

Communication between school counselors, teachers, and administrators with a foster child's social worker can be paramount in times of emergency in regard to the foster child's behavior, or even academic understanding. For example, Derrick is a 15-year-old foster child. Derrick had been physically and verbally abused by his parents for much of his young life, before being abandoned by them. Derrick suffers from bouts of rage and is prone to outbursts of anger over what many might consider small or trivial matters. Longing to fit in and shed his "foster kid" label, Derrick often tries to be the center of attention in his classrooms, as well as in the school cafeteria during lunchtime.

One lunch period in particular, Derrick was asked to quiet down by a school administrator. Struggling with the swirling emotions that were churning within him, Derrick lashed out in anger toward the administrator, swearing, and even throwing a chair across the cafeteria. After a great deal of time had passed, Derrick was removed from the cafeteria and placed into a conference room, where the troubled student began to talk about suicide. As the school had been informed that Derrick was in foster care two weeks prior, when he enrolled into the school, the school administrator attempted to contact the student's social worker in order to not only inform the social worker of the situation but also to receive some guidance and suggestions on the matter. However, attempts to do so did not meet with success, leaving the school administrators and counselor ill-prepared on how best to address Derrick's behavioral needs. Unfortunately, in times of emergency such as this, often teachers and school officials are unable to contact a social worker, leaving teachers and administrators forced to attend to the issue on their own.

Social workers

As noted earlier, social workers today are often under-resourced, underpaid, overworked, and overwhelmed. Budget cuts have made a difficult job even more so for those social workers who work with children in foster care. With the decrease in funding comes the decrease also in the number of social workers employed by an agency. Yet, as the number of social workers decreases, the number of children placed in foster care remains the same. As a result, the responsibilities of a social worker are increasing, as they take on more roles and caseloads. Consequently, social workers are finding that they have "to do more with less" (University of Connecticut 2011).

Social workers, as we examined in Chapter 1, truly do have a great many responsibilities when it comes to the children in foster care that are assigned to them. Finding foster homes for children, medical concerns of the children, working with birth parents, attending court, and working with foster parents are just part of their daily task loads. Further, one of the more important roles they may play, or should play, is that of ensuring that the child's educational needs are met. This may include helping to plan the student's course load and classes, monitoring school behavior and academic performance, and communicating with teachers on a regular basis.

To begin with, when a foster child is enrolled into a new school, it is often the responsibility of the social worker to make certain that the transcripts are delivered and in order. Often, without these transcripts, schools are unable to allow a student to enroll into the school. What many foster parents, schools, and society in general fail to realize, though, is that social workers have many children to look after. Thus, they are unable to focus all of their time and attention on just one child. Of course, while social workers have similar mandates in regard to how they attend to the needs of a child, there are instances where the needs of a particular child may require further attention, thus taking up time from another. The placement of a child into a new home and school is certainly an instance that requires a great amount of time, as there is so much to do yet so little time to do it in. For the busy and overwhelmed social worker, tracking down transcripts from the past school may be a task that is not an easy one to do. Some schools are quicker to respond to this request than others. While some schools may be able to fax, scan, or email the transcripts of a former student to another school, other schools may require that the transcripts be picked up by a parent or social worker and delivered to the new school in person. Unfortunately, an overwhelmed and busy social worker may not be able to attend to this immediately. As a result, the child may not be placed into a school immediately, and may indeed miss a few days or more as the new school waits for the transcripts from the previous school:

> One of the hardest parts of my job is working with schools. When one of my foster kiddos is placed into a new school, I often don't have the time to get to that new school and meet any of the teachers, school counselor, or others. Many times, I have to rely on the foster parents to make sure that the new school has all the paperwork they need, including transcripts. There is just not enough time in the day to get all that we need to get done.

> LAURI M., SOCIAL WORKER OF 7 YEARS

As Lauri mentioned here, many times social workers have to rely on their foster parents to assist with registering for school, monitoring grades, evaluating the foster child's behavior and performance, and even assuring that the child is having any academic special needs met, including that of tutoring. One study found that the involvement of social workers is limited a great deal to simply dealing with the behavioral problems of the children while in school (Finkelstein, Wamsley, and Miranda 2002).

While some social workers took steps to become actively involved in the foster child's school performance, the same study found that many social workers chose not to become involved in the day-to-day activities and performance of the student, or were not aware of any problems until they arose, thus necessitating involvement on their behalf.

There are also those occasions when social workers are unable to receive the information they need from the foster parents they are working with. According to the study by Finkelstein *et al.* (2002), some foster parents cannot be relied upon to provide report cards and behavior reports to the social worker. Some schools are no more helpful in this regard, either. For many social workers, a large amount of time may pass before obtaining the report cards and school grades, delaying close monitoring of the foster child's progress by those social workers who wish to remain involved. Social workers also may have a difficult time getting in contact with teachers and school administrators. Busy teachers and school counselors may not find time to meet social workers about grades and behavior, as well as any important Individual Education Plans (IEPs) that may be planned for the foster student; meetings that could be quite beneficial in planning to best meet the student's needs and necessary resources. For many foster children, a social worker is the most consistent adult in the child's life, and may be more aware of the child's needs than a foster parent, as foster children are often moved from home to home. A social worker's input and professional opinion can be crucial in coordinating meeting all the needs of the child. However, as there is a high rate of social worker turnover (Stephenson 2009), it may be difficult for new social workers to be up-to-date with a foster child's academic needs.

Foster parents

One of the most important keys for a foster child's success in school is the support, involvement, and encouragement from his or her foster parents. Indeed, according to teachers in one study, those children in foster care whose foster parents are involved in their school activities perform better in regard to academic achievements (Coulling 2000). Unfortunately, many foster parents are not involved with their foster child's school, for a variety of reasons.

Many foster parents are under the false belief that their foster children have no unique or distinctive problems while in school due to their being placed into the foster care system. Furthermore, one study found that many foster parents believed that their foster children were performing well in a social fashion, and that they had many friends. Along with this, foster parents in this study also were of the belief that their foster children were not embarrassed or even stigmatized by being placed into foster care (Finkelstein et al. 2002). As a result, many foster parents are not overly concerned about their foster child's school performance. Additionally, some foster parents may be satisfied with their foster child simply passing the class with an average grade. Yet, as we have clearly seen in previous chapters, children in foster care very much do suffer from various emotional traumas while in school, perform at a lower level academically than their peers, and often feel stigmatized by the label placed upon them as a foster child. Such complacent foster parents are therefore doing a great disservice to their foster children, as well as to the school as a whole.

Often, foster parents do not seek out or initiate contact with teachers or school employees regarding the student. In fact, much of the conversation between the two is initiated by teachers, largely in response to the student's behavior (Finkelstein *et al.* 2002). Many of today's foster parents have already had children graduate from high school, or have never had biological children of their own. As a result, a large number of these foster parents do not recognize the importance of reaching out to a student's teachers on a regular basis in order to stay up-to-date with grades and performance, or may not be familiar with school policies and procedures on how to do this. There are also foster parents who have numerous foster children placed in their home, along with their own biological children and the addition of their own job, so they may simply not have enough time in their day to reach out to teachers and school employees in regard to the child's behavior and grades.

Foster children often suffer from a number of medical conditions, requiring them to spend large amounts of time in a doctor's office, resulting in even more absences from the classroom. As a result, foster parents may have to take time off from their own workplace, attending to doctor's appointments for their foster child. At times, some foster parents may become upset with a child's school for not being understanding enough in cases such as these (Finkelstein *et al.* 2002). In addition to these types of school absences, there are those absences related to school transfers, as we have noted earlier. Some foster parents may wait until the beginning of a new school year, in the belief that they should not disrupt both the school and the child's education, resulting in the child falling even further behind.

As we have clearly seen, there are many factors inhibiting a foster child from succeeding in school. Whether it is the emotional traumas the child may be struggling with, the multiple displacements from home to home and school to school, or the lack of understanding from social workers, school employees, and foster parents, children in foster care have numerous obstacles preventing them from performing well. In order for our children to not only survive, but to succeed in school, it is vital that all three parties understand these obstacles, and work together for the benefit of these troubled children.

CHAPTER 6

Expectations of a Foster Child While in School

Upon hearing this young man's background, I immediately had a visceral reaction.

Neglect. Abandonment. Abuse. These had been just words to me. Words that I knew were tragic and deplorable, but still just words. Coming from a relatively stable home and family, I had never lived through these words. I had never seen what these words look like in someone's life. I had never realized just how tragic and deplorable they were.

As the foster parent explained this young man's experiences at home, I became stuck on the images that were being shared with me. I felt sick, disgusted, repulsed, and angry. How could a parent allow his or her children to be physically abused? To live in an environment where a mound of feces is piled into a room? To allow the children's clothes, skin, and hair to be contaminated with harmful bacteria from the feces? How could a parent put drugs above the love and care of his or her children?

As a parent myself, I was speechless.

The foster parent then revealed to me that this young man had been in my school system before but had received major disciplinary actions. According to the foster parent, this was his last chance. I was to inform the foster parent immediately if I had any problems with behavior or academic performance.

The last thing the foster parent told me was that the kid was brilliant, identified early as a recipient of gifted services through the school system.

Of course, I had heard that before. Many parents extoll the virtues of their children when we meet. So, I took this last statement somewhat casually. In my mind, I was still nonplussed about the young man's home life.

But when I met this young man in class, I immediately recognized his brilliance. He picked up concepts extremely quickly.

He was able to make inferences and draw conclusions almost instantaneously. He had read or was familiar with novels and writers that no other ninth grader was familiar with. In short, he was an excellent reader and critical thinker.

However, he was quite obnoxious and impulsive. He was fidgety and loud. He was devious and surreptitious. He often said whatever came to his mind. He tapped his pencil on his desk to the consternation of others. He jumped over rows of desks to find his seat instead of walking around the other desks. He threw balls of paper across the room into the trashcan. He made lewd comments while reading *Romeo and Juliet*. He played with his phone during tests and quizzes. And although I could never prove it, I'm absolutely certain he told me bold-face lies about where he was when he was missing or why work wasn't turned in on time.

While many teachers would use these behaviors as evidence for the need of behavior referrals, I was willing to overlook much of them. Very rarely did they disrupt the class enough for me to make a formal complaint. On rare occurrences, I informed the foster parent of the behavior. Generally, however, all I needed to do was look at him and shake my head or ask him to calm down in the hallway.

The few times I did need to talk to him in the hallway, this young man became immediately penitent. He was respectful, saying, "Yes, sir" or "No, sir." He looked me in the eyes and told me he was sorry. Once back in the classroom, he would give me no more problems, at least until the next day.

I was willing to do this because of the potential in this kid. A potential that was so close to being wasted by his biological parents. A potential that needed sympathy and tolerance instead of Eichmannism and rigidity. I saw this young man entering Harvard or Brown University one day, and quite frankly, I was afraid his future might be one administrative referral away from being crushed.

BRIAN P., ENGLISH TEACHER OF 5 YEARS

The moment a foster child is placed into a new home and a new school, their whole world has changed. There are now different rules and different expectations to follow for them. Their foster home and school are new environments for them. There is even a set of new parents for them, as well as a school full of new teachers and fellow classmates. Everything they have known to be true is now different. These are significant changes in the child's lifestyle. All decision making has been taken away from them. They are in their new foster home and new school against their own will, against their own choice.

Foster children typically perform poorly in school for a variety of reasons. Multiple displacement from home to home often results in foster children becoming dissatisfied with school, and quickly losing interest. Transcripts and school records are often missing or incomplete when a student enrolls into a new school, many times resulting in the children not being enrolled in classes designed to best help them, nor having the resources they need to succeed. Along with this, teachers and administrators are often not aware that the student is a foster child, nor aware of the many emotional difficulties and traumas that foster children face, in general. Then there are the difficulties the child may have faced while living with their birth family members. They may never have had rules of any kind in their home, nor had the responsibility of doing chores. Homework may be something completely foreign to them, as it may not have been expected or enforced. Manners may not have been taught or modeled in their family. Even personal hygiene may not have been established before they came to live with their new foster family. Without a doubt, children in foster care are likely to struggle in school, whether it is with academic studies, behavior, social relationships, or a combination of the three.

Those adults and caregivers who are working with children who are placed into foster care need to set reasonable expectations with the students, remembering where they came from and what they are going through on a daily basis. To begin with, it will be important that adults set realistic academic expectations. As we have examined, children in foster care are very likely to suffer from poor grades and learning disabilities. Often, this is due to the fact that roughly 50 percent of foster children change schools at least four times after initially beginning their formal education at age five or six (Powers and Stotland 2002). With these children, it often takes four to six months to recover academically after each placement disruption, or moving from school to school (Calvin 2001). For this simple reason alone, as well as the numerous others documented earlier, it is easy to understand why foster children regularly perform poorly academically.

Parental expectations can be defined as "realistic beliefs or judgments that parents have about their children's future achievement as reflected in course grades, highest level of schooling attained, or college attendance" (Yamamoto and Holloway 2010). These expectations by parents are a strong predictor of how a child will perform while in school (Davis-Kean 2005). Furthermore, high expectations by parents positively affect not only the child's academic performance, but also their school attendance (Jeynes 2005). Indeed, these parental expectations often have strong effects on their children's academic performance, school behavior, and their motivation to succeed. Yet, many children come from homes where there are little to no such expectations of them, and children in foster care are likely to fall into this category. Sadly, for many of these children, no one has held them up to any sort of expectations, thus they are also likely to not have high expectations of themselves.

Teachers, foster parents, and social workers should place reasonable expectations on a foster child, not only of their academic performance, but also of their behavior and social skills. After determining where the child's academic level of performance is at, and what the child is capable of, adults need to ensure that they do not demand too much. These expectations must be reasonable and realistic. After all, each child is different, every child learns differently, and not every child is bound for Harvard or Oxford after high school. Children in foster care, as we have seen, perform at a lower academic level than their peers, for a variety of reasons. This fact alone needs to be remembered by those who care for them. Indeed, these caregivers should not expect school to be the focus of the children's young lives, as it is not. This is important to bear in mind with children in foster care, as they are likely not going to strive for academic excellence or place school work as a priority in their lives. A large number of these students just may not care about their school work, their grades, or how they behave in school. This will not change magically overnight once a child is placed into a foster home. Indeed, it may take a long time for a student in foster care to change their attitude toward school after they are placed into a foster home. In fact, they may not change their attitude toward school at all while under the supervision of foster care, or even for the rest of their life. This may be due to the fact that the child had lived in an environment or home for many years where school was not stressed as important. To that end, teachers, social workers, and foster parents need to be aware of this possibility.

Stages of reading

As we saw in Chapter 3, children in foster care are often behind in their reading skills. Indeed, many of them have a smaller vocabulary, and fewer experiences of reading aloud to adults and parents, than children from traditional homes. Furthermore, many students from foster care also have not had adults read to them aloud. Thus, it will be necessary that foster parents, and other caregivers in their lives, do not place high expectations on these children immediately when it comes to reading skills. In order to better understand the child's struggles with reading, it is important to have some appreciation of the stages of reading development that children experience. These stages of development, designed by pioneering Harvard researcher Jeanne S. Chall, can give foster parents, teachers, and social workers insight into where the child is at in regard to reading skills, as well as knowledge on how to best help them. Chall (1983) also attached ages and grade levels to these reading development stages.

Stage 0. Pre-reading: birth to 6 years

In this initial stage, children are learning how to read through the act of pretending. It is in this stage that children learn about the sounds of language. These young readers "read" a book by retelling the story in their own words by looking at the pictures, or by retelling what was read to them previously. Recognition of letters of the alphabet begins during this stage, as children begin to name aloud the letters they see. Children also show signs of beginning to print or write down letters they see, as well as their own name.

Finally, these young readers also learn to play with books, pencils, paper, and crayons during this beginning stage.

Stage 1. Initial reading and decoding: 6–7 years of age

For most children, this is the stage where they learn to read, becoming young readers. At the beginning, these young readers learn the relation between letters and sounds, connecting the two together to sound out and decode words. These young children also learn to recognize the relation between the printed word and spoken word. It is at this stage where children are able to read simple text which contains high-frequency words. Young readers also are able to use their skills and insight in order to "sound out" words and syllables that are new to them.

Stage 2. Confirmation and fluency: 7–8 years of age

During this stage, children begin to recognize whole words automatically without having to sound out each letter aloud. Indeed, these readers begin to read simple, familiar stories and selections with increasing confidence and fluency. It is during this phase in the child's reading level where their mind has the space for higher-level concepts and for more developed and complex stories.

Stage 3. Reading for learning: 9–13 years of age

At this level, the child has become a fluent and confident reader. It is as this point where children begin to read to learn, acquiring knowledge and information in the process. Along with this, readers at this stage read to gain new experiences, feelings, and attitudes. In order to be successful at this stage in their reading development, children will need to draw upon their own background experiences in order to fully understand the new information they are reading and exposed to. In Stage 3, many foster children begin to experience difficulties. Due to the various impoverished backgrounds they originate from, these children may not have the life experiences they need in order to relate to and put into context what they are reading.

Stage 4. Multiple viewpoints: 15–17 years of age

It is at this stage that students are reading a wide and broad range of complex material, analyzing and critiquing what they read throughout the process. Many of the texts they read have a variety of viewpoints, and readers learn how to understand multiple viewpoints through what they read. Indeed, it is at this stage that these students are able to amend any previous thoughts or beliefs they might have had if the new material they are reading should counter theses beliefs and prove them incorrect.

Stage 5. Construction and reconstruction: 18 years and beyond

In this advanced stage, reading is used for one's own purposes, such as personal and professional. Readers at this level read to construct knowledge by taking information from a mixture of sources, interpreting it to create new knowledge. Readers in Stage 5 also use the art of skimming to read some passages in a rapid process. Finally, these readers form their own educated viewpoints and opinions based upon the material they read.

Behavior

There are many factors as to why a child in foster care might have behavioral issues while in school. Perhaps they were never encouraged to behave in their own home, and have never been taught the importance of behaving in the classroom by their biological family members. The child may be lashing out in the classroom due to the emotional trauma they are facing. They might be frustrated due to the fact that they have been put into the wrong classes after being placed into care. They may suffer from physical and/or psychological problems that contribute to learning problems, causing further frustrations. Schools may contribute to their behavior problems by not implanting the proper school-based behavior modification practices needed to best meet the child's needs. Teachers may also not be aware of the best teaching or behavioral modifications needed for the child's needs. Visitations and court appearances may also contribute to behavior issues while in school. Peer pressure and the stigma or status of being a foster child may lead to issues of behavior while in school, too. Along with all this, the child may be embarrassed if personal and private information is released about their status and/or their family members, which might include mental illness, poverty, drug use and addictions, and criminal background and imprisonment. This type of embarrassment may also lead to behavior problems in the school, as the child's anxieties increase and relationships with their fellow students are threatened. Whatever the reason or reasons might be, children in foster care, as noted in Chapter 3, suffer from a number of behavioral-related issues while in school, as they simply try to survive the trauma and challenges faced while being placed into foster care.

For foster parents, school employees, and social workers, it will be necessary to keep these behavioral issues in mind in regard to the child. When a child is first placed into a foster home, and into a new school and classroom, these caregivers should not expect the child to act and behave in a way that reflects the model student. Indeed, the child is likely not to behave in a way that is ideal or appropriate. Therefore, social workers, teachers, and foster parents need to be expectant of this, as well as prepared for if and when issues of behavior might arise. As with academic performance, expectations must be both realistic and reasonable in this regard. Along with this, foster parents and teachers, as well as social workers, must be understanding when those times arise where the student falls back into a familiar pattern. Take the story of Jonathan, for example:

Jonathan was our 13-year-old foster child, and had lived with us for just over a year. Before Jonathan came to live with our family, he was always in trouble in school. He was often in fights in school with fellow students, spoke back to his teachers in a rude way, and would often use curse words and profanity when talking to others. When he lived with his biological family members, Jonathan would miss many days of school in a row, and was absent a lot. He also spent a lot of time in the school's detention center, when he was in school.

My husband and I held Jonathan to high expectations with his behavior. His grades were average, and we did not demand more than he was able. With his behavior, though, we told him that we expected him to be on his best behavior every day. The first few months were hard, as he continued to get into trouble. As the months passed, though, Jonathan's behavior improved, and he was doing great in school, and not getting into trouble.

One afternoon, the vice principal at his school called my work to tell me that Jonathan would be spending the next day in the school's I.S.S. (In School Suspension). Apparently, our foster child had hit another student. When his teacher asked him about it, Jonathan became defensive and started to argue with his teacher, which got him into further trouble. When he came home that night, we talked to Jonathan about his behavior, about what was right and what was wrong. Considering where he had come from it was no surprise that he would slip back into his familiar pattern once in a while. I mean, this is how he was raised. It is going to take a lot of work to help him change his ways, and it isn't going to happen overnight. We just have to be patient with him.

ANGELA, FOSTER PARENT OF 7 YEARS

CHAPTER 7

How Teachers Can Help

Many years ago friends of mine opened their home to become foster parents. I have watched many young people pass through their home, which is filled with love and siblings and animals and caring parents. Several of these children I was fortunate to know on two fronts: the home side which was trying to be loving and caring, and the classroom side that could be anything but loving and caring. I tried to find ways to help these students maneuver through those hard and difficult days. What I found was that each child, no matter the situation, was missing that feeling of belonging and being loved.

These experiences helped me to realize a few things about foster children in the classroom. First I had to draw on Maslow's Hierarchy Chart. These students have so many things going on that learning the vocabulary list for my class was the last thing on their minds. Secondly, I realize that there were some major trust issues going on with these children. They are always waiting for the "other shoe" to drop. So while in my class they are not always so concerned about the subject area I had to offer. Also with these students I had to be concerned with a new group of people...the foster parents. These are not the same as the biological parents, of course. They are different in ways like trying to form relationships with this child that was placed in their home with no prior connection. For them education was not the most important reality in their home. This fact made me more aware that maybe homework did not need to carry so much weight for this child. I had to think of ways of getting the work done so that "family" time at night was not always spent arguing over homework. Again, other things in the foster home had to be handled and worked on more than my homework assignment. In the families I have worked with I had to accept the fact that things had to be done a little differently. These are children who want to fit in and be accepted, but they have the whole issue of having to learn to trust these people in ways that the teacher may not understand. They want to have friends to talk to, but how much do they share with this new person? How will this person take what they are told? They need to trust that their worlds are not going to be turned upside down again. As their teachers we have to try to make their days in our classrooms as welcoming, encouraging, and understanding for as long as the student is there. We must encourage them to trust us.

One of my students was adopted by her foster parents so her world became more settled but her story did not run smoothly. This student was taken from her home as a pre-teen and she was very angry. She was angry at her biological mom for letting this horrible thing happen to her. She was angry with the foster family for being there. She was angry at the social workers, who were looking out for her best interests. She was angry at the school for not being her old school. She was angry at herself for not being "good" enough for this not to happen to her. So this young girl came to my class wanting, and needing, to be angry. I had to learn how to get her to try to put the anger away, or at least find a place to put it.

I remember the days she would come to class without her homework done, having not studied for a test, and with an attitude as big as the moon. Being in my class that day was the last place she wanted to be. This happened after a day where her lessons were well prepared and she made a one hundred on a pop quiz. So what had changed? Court...she had had to go to a hearing and had seen her mother. This was such a traumatic experience it threw her off for days. I could only imagine what her life with the foster family was like for a while after that. As a teacher I had to dig past the anger to find what changes were happening in this child's life. It helped when the foster parents kept me in the loop about visits or court days, because I could almost plan for when one of these visits happened my sweet young lady would turn into an angry withdrawn person. It helped to be prepared for these events.

This student knew my door was open to her and that I was there, but I still had to reassure her of this fact. As she went through high school she became more at ease with other students and soon developed friendships. She began to trust more and let the walls down a little bit at a time. As her teacher I found myself watching from the sidelines, ready to try to steer her in a different direction, if needed. She would become unsure of where she fit in, and lived for a long time afraid that she was going to be taken away from this home. I believe that many times she did not accept people who wanted to be her friend out of self-protection. It is not perfect, nor is it easy to be her friend.

Foster children are not always in the mindset for education and I had to learn that was ok, too. I know that there were many things that did not stick with these students from my lessons. I hope that what I did helped them develop some of those skills they needed to relearn as they entered my class. Much to my concern my student did not always make the right decisions and most of the time these decisions were made in an effort to fit in with the "crowd." After many ups and downs, and many still to come, this young girl did go on to find success and happiness in her own way. I know that she does still carry many scars from these experiences, many that I do not know anything about, but with the help of her parents she has found a way to trust and is making a life for herself.

Isn't that what we hope for *all* our students?

JOHNNIE SUE M., TEACHER OF 30 YEARS

For eight hours a day or more, and for five days a week for much of a calendar year, a foster child will spend their time in school. Indeed, children in foster care will most likely spend more of their time each day with teachers than they will with their foster parents. As we have seen, though, many foster children would rather be any place else other than in school, as it is a constant reminder that they are just that, a foster child. Yet, teachers and school employees have the opportunity to help foster children in a unique and positive manner.

When a foster child is placed into a teacher's classroom, it will benefit all involved if the teacher is given some information and insight into the child. Teachers, as well as school counselors, often do not have the background information they might need when having a foster child under their supervision. In most cases, the background information is not permitted to be released due to issues of confidentiality through legal acts of protection. It may also be to prevent teachers from forming an opinion about the student as a foster child, and from lowering the expectations of the child, both academically and in behavior. However, with information comes understanding. Many times, this information is necessary for a teacher in order to fully understand the student's needs and abilities. The more information a teacher may have on the child, the better equipped the teacher becomes when trying to aid the child in his or her behavior and academic performance. If teachers have some insight into a child's past experiences, these teachers may become more compassionate and understanding toward the child. School counselors can help teachers by delivering as much information about the foster child as possible to the student's teachers prior to the student's arrival into the class, or as soon as possible after. In the same manner, teachers can also request information from the school counselor regarding the foster child.

With this understanding and compassion comes patience and tolerance for any behavioral problems the child may have. If a foster child should lash out in anger or frustration toward the teacher or other students, due to the myriad of emotions the child is struggling to deal with, teachers are better equipped to handle the child's emotional turmoil. This background information and insight can be most helpful as teachers consider how to best handle the situation. Instead of quickly writing a behavior referral on the child's conduct, sending the child immediately to the principal's office, or placing the student in a detention hall of some kind, teachers can find other methods to first respond to the behavior issues. Meet the student outside the classroom, perhaps standing near the classroom door, welcoming the foster child with a pleasant word before they enter the room. By doing so, teachers are able to be proactive, as they look for possible signs of any problems before the student enters the room. If the student looks agitated or upset, take a moment to talk to the student, asking if he is all right, and giving words of positive encouragement, aiding in diffusing any problems that might arise.

Foster children often have difficulty with trust issues when it comes to adults, as well as building a healthy relationship with an adult figure. Thus, the relationships between teachers and foster children are quite often unhealthy ones. Therefore, it is important to keep in mind that the foster child may have experienced harsh words, yelling, and abuse from the hands of adults. Instead, teachers should approach foster children with a calm voice, a composed attitude, and with tolerance. The more one argues, the more the child's agitation is likely to increase. Have the foster child sit away from those students who are distracting or mean-spirited. If the student should begin to demonstrate behavior that is not appropriate in the classroom, walk over to the student, and give them a gentle reminder or warning. If the behavior should persist, allow the student to have a brief time-out of three to ten minutes, where they can sit in a quiet corner of the room, step outside, or go and work in another classroom or school library/media center as they collect their thoughts and try to calm down. If need be, encourage the student to visit the school counselor, where they can discuss the issues facing their behavior and emotional confusion. If problems continue, teachers should have a brief conference with the student to discuss the student's behavior in the classroom, and how it is presenting a problem to the classroom environment and learning process as a whole. Along with this, teachers can ask open-ended questions, allowing the student the opportunity to discuss their behavior. Working alongside the foster child, teachers can then discuss solutions to the behavior problem, asking the student for their own suggestions. If these means are not effective, the teacher can then ask to have a behavior conference with the foster parents, social worker, and other school officials, if need be.

One of the greatest ways a teacher can help a foster child is with academic understanding. Many teachers expect good grades and school performance to be a priority in the lives of the majority of their students. Yet, for children in foster care, school is not a priority, and is not a focus. Rather, the main focus and priority for many students who are placed into foster homes is that of survival; survival from moving from home to home, survival from the abuse and neglect they may have faced in their lives, survival from living apart from their other family members, and survival from moving from school to school. As foster children are often behind academically, as well as struggle with the fact that they are coming from outside school districts with different expectations, teachers need to be conscious of this fact. There are sure to be gaps in learning and disabilities due to the instability and multiple displacements. In addition, foster children struggle with many personal and emotional issues while in the foster home, and homework is often not the main objective while in the home each evening. Instead, the emotional issues your child faces may take center stage on a particular evening. Teachers need to assign homework with this in mind, being sensitive to their issues. School educators should avoid assigning school tasks and projects that are insensitive to children in foster care. These might include projects which ask for students to write about a mother or father before Mother's/Father's Day, bringing in pictures from home, tracing a family tree, or reporting on a family member who is an inspiration.

Along with this, teachers should be aware when assigning homework of whether there is someone who is at home who can be of help and assistance. Teachers can also create lesson plans with these foster parents and caregivers in mind and engage in daily conversation that incorporates the student. Finally, teachers can be of tremendous help to both foster children and foster parents by allowing flexibility on deadlines and due dates for homework, as well as quizzes and test-taking, particularly when assigning homework or test dates around visitations with birth parents and biological family members. Often, children in care are filled with various anxieties on the day of a visitation, as well as the following day, as they try to process the swirling emotions that come with visiting with someone who may have neglected or abused them, or a family member in jail. Furthermore, sometimes these visitations lead to false promises and false hopes of being reunited soon with birth family members; promises and hopes that leave the children incapable of completing homework and studying for quizzes and tests in an appropriate and focused manner.

Flexibility and understanding with homework and testing is also important with children in foster care as they are likely to face more absences than the traditional student. Days will not only be missed because of visitations, which may take place during school hours, but also due to doctor's appointments. As noted earlier, many children in foster care suffer from various medical conditions and needs. Children who are placed into a foster home for the first time may spend large amounts of time in doctor's appointments, as it may be the first time they have visited the doctor in a long period of time, or perhaps the first time ever. Children in care may also have to be absent from school in order to attend a meeting with a therapist. Along with this, foster care students may also be absent from school due to court appearances. There are occasions where foster children have to appear in court, such as permanency hearings, which are often court-mandated, as well as other hearings involving the child and the case. As court is generally held during school hours, the child will most likely be absent from school for these. In all of these scenarios, teachers need to be more understanding when assigning homework and test dates, allowing for more time and a flexible schedule to complete school work and test-taking. Teachers can also help students in foster care with after-school help with any homework, and areas the child might be struggling with.

Sadly, many children in care have never had a positive adult role model in their life. Along with this, they have never had encouragement from a caring adult, either. There was no one who would tell the child that he or she was doing a good job; no one who was lifting them up in praise; no one who told them that the sky was the limit for them. Quite simply, there was no one who believed in the child. Instead, these children were yelled at and cursed by the adults in their lives for long periods each day; never expected to work on their school work; discouraged at every attempt to succeed; and belittled and ridiculed by those who were supposed to love them the most. Foster parents and social workers have the opportunity to be a caring and positive role model in the child's life, and often are; however, the child is going to spend more time with their teachers than any other adult while in foster care. Therefore, teachers should be as encouraging as possible to students in foster care. Even the smallest step forward and any minor advances in progress by the student should be noted and celebrated by the teacher, in regard to both academic performance and behavior. After all, children placed in foster care may never have had an encouraging word said toward them before, and may suffer from a sense of low self-esteem, or little self-worth. Praise for an accomplishment, no matter how small, by a teacher can be most effective in aiding in the development and even the healing of the student.

For some children in care, a teacher may be the one person the child feels comfortable talking with, sharing their stories of pain and emotional turmoil. Those teachers who are open to being a listening ear to children in foster care are those teachers who have the opportunity to make a significant impact in the life of a troubled child. At the same time, if the child should relate some information that an administrator or counselor should be aware of, it is necessary that the teacher informs those school employees immediately.

Positive and strong personal rapport between teachers and students at risk is important not only for a student's academic success, but also for the student's behavioral success. Positive relationships with teachers give foster care students a sense of belonging and connectedness to a school, especially for those students who are moving from school to school due to placements into new foster homes. Teachers need training and professional development in regard to establishing rapport with students at risk. This training can give teachers a number of strategies designed to establish a positive relationship with these foster children. Teachers can attempt to establish a positive and friendly rapport with a student at risk in a number of ways, including reading emotional cues from students and responding to them in a non-judgmental fashion. Teachers should be alert and observant for any emotional problems or outbursts that might occur, anticipating them and acting in a proactive fashion.

Children in foster care often have a difficult time with social skills due to the personal traumas they may have faced before coming into care. As a result, these students may find it difficult to interact with their peers, and instead choose not to become socially involved for fear of receiving additional trauma (Kools 1999). Sadly, many students in foster care do not have any friends in school, or experience feelings of animosity toward their peers. Outbursts of anger are common in these children toward both their teachers and their peers (Finkelstein *et al.* 2002). Teachers can assist these troubled students in helping them develop appropriate and adequate social skills, and at the same time encourage the student to become more involved in the school with clubs and organizations, music, sports, and other extra-curricular activities.

Advocacy is another way teachers can help foster students. Indeed, teachers and other school personnel need to remember that many children in foster care have never had an adult looking after them, throughout much of their lives. A teacher, school counselor, administrator, or other school employee might just be the first adult fighting for the child to have a better life, championing the child's needs. School employees have the distinct opportunity of changing a foster child's life like no other adult in a positive fashion in this manner.

As we have seen, students in foster care may not be enrolled in the right classes and courses when first enrolling into school, due to lack of records and transcripts. As a result, these new students may be placed in the wrong classes as schools merely attempt to place the foster child into a classroom. Let us examine one foster care student from a middle school classroom:

Jake was a foster student placed into a low-level middle school Literature class I taught when he first moved to our school. He was placed in the class on the assumption by the school that he was a foster child and that his skills were most likely low. Yet, the student was far more advanced than his fellow classmates, and was in fact remarkably bright. Jake scored quite high initially upon placement into the class on homework assignments and spelling quizzes, and was far and away ahead of all the other students. He quickly lost interest in the class, though, due to the lack of learning he faced each day. As a result of not being challenged by the class, he began to behave in a disruptive manner.

This all happened within the first week of Jake being placed into my classroom. One day, in his second week in our school, I took him aside, and asked him to take a test, by himself, one that I gave all the other students at the end of the year; a test that was able to better measure whether he truly needed to be in my class, or not. Not surprisingly, Jake scored incredibly high. I asked Jake's other teachers how he was doing, and a pattern became clear. He just wasn't being challenged in any of his classes, and was beginning to act out. I was able to convince the school counselor to have Jake tested, and we found out that instead of the low-level academic course, he should have been placed in the gifted classes, for those who were advanced. Now, Jake is getting all A's, loves his classes, and is not a discipline problem, at all. I feel that we got to him just in time.

MICHELLE A., TEACHER

In this case, Jake's teacher acted as an advocate for him. When Michelle noticed that the foster child was placed into the wrong class, she quickly acted to ensure that he was having his educational needs met, advocating for his needs. Many times, children in foster care are placed into classes that are too difficult and advanced for them, thus causing them to struggle as they are so far behind academically. Between 30 and 40 percent of all children placed in foster care are also in special education courses, and are eligible for special educational services (Christian 2003). Like Michelle, these teachers can also be an advocate for those students who are placed into classes that surpass their abilities, and ensure that they are instead placed into the appropriate classes. More than anyone else, teachers are able to determine whether or not a foster child is placed in the correct course and classroom, and can act as an advocate for these children in this regard. Many foster children benefit from guidance counseling, and the teacher can aid in this by observing the student in the classroom and informing the school counselor and foster parents of any emotional difficulties the child might be suffering from.

As we saw in Chapter 4, children in foster care face many challenges when aging out of the system. Tragically, the majority of children in foster care never see the day when they walk across a stage, receiving a high school diploma. Along with this, the number that actually attends college, if even for a short time, is staggeringly small. Teachers need to stress the importance of education and encourage the child to graduate from high school, with the possibility of college, technical school, or military service as important subsequent options. As many aged-out foster youth cannot afford college, assistance in this manner is most helpful. Educational communities can begin a foster scholarship fund, setting up a college fund for those foster children wishing to further their education. Supplies for school can be donated to school systems who work with children who will soon age out.

These supplies can include paper, pencils, pens, calculators, backpacks, and other school needs. For those who are enrolled in college, bookstore gift cards and certificates can also be quite beneficial, and educators can assist by donating many of these items.

Teachers need to develop a positive, strong, and healthy relationship with both the student's foster parents and social workers. As we have seen, social workers are very busy, as are teachers, and may not find time to reach out to the school. There are also those foster parents who will not reach out to schools to check on their foster child's academic and behavior status, for whatever reason. Therefore, it will be up to the teacher to reach out to the foster parents in this regard. Indeed, it is imperative that teachers and schools know who the foster parents and caregivers are. Teachers can invite both social workers and teachers to visit the school, attend parent/teacher conferences, and become involved in school events and activities, such as volunteering. Furthermore, they can invite all adults involved with the child to attend any and all meetings involving the child, assuring the child that their opinion and viewpoint are both important and necessary. It is important for teachers to seek out the advice of those professionals that are working with the child, and to involve them in planning educational resources and support.

Anytime a child in foster care is disruptive in class, or behaves in a way that is not appropriate within the classroom and school environment, teachers, counselors, and/or school administrators should contact both foster parents and social workers, whenever possible. Whether it is a phone call, an email, or a text message, foster parents and social workers need to know how the child is behaving. The teachers and educators can thus seek out opinions and advice from both foster parents and social workers when dealing with a foster child's behavior. These adults may be familiar with specific strategies for the child in regard to behavior modification. In the same vein, teachers can also relay any good news to foster parents and social workers in regard to the child's behavior in the classroom and school generally. This will allow these caregivers the opportunity to not only praise the child for their good behavior, but to also encourage them to continue with it. Teachers can provide these adults with progress reports and grade status, with perhaps weekly updates and other notices. As any teacher knows, the more information the caregiver has about the child, as well as the more involved the caregiver and parent is, the more active and supportive they are with both the child and the school.

Far too many times, foster parents and social workers are simply not aware of the numerous and varied special programs that schools offer. Foster children might benefit tremendously from special educational courses, as well as after-school tutoring and remedial programs, all intended to help struggling students. Teachers can help these caregivers to access these special education services and support programs. Along with this, teachers and educators can also direct foster parents and social workers to support groups and agencies that are designed to help children with particular types of disabilities. Helpful websites and other educational resources should also be pointed out to the caregivers of troubled students by teachers and school employees.

More than anyone else, teachers are aware of how important education and a high school degree are for all children. Without a doubt, teachers can make a tremendous impact in the life of a child in foster care. Teachers are often in a position to be a positive role model and influence for these students in care. In addition, teachers can also help provide foster parents and social workers with the help they need when meeting a foster child's educational needs. With some planning, understanding, and guidance, teachers can make the difference between failure and success for a child in foster care.

CHAPTER 8

How Foster Parents Can Help

Caleb is a seven-year-old boy in the second grade. He and his older brother came into foster care due to extreme neglect. The brothers lived in a filthy, drug-filled home with very little to eat; often they could be found wandering the streets asking neighbors for scraps of food. The Department of Family and Children Services was called after Caleb's brother called 911 after witnessing his mother get stabbed in the neck by her abusive boyfriend.

Six months later, Caleb and his brother arrived at our home after three failed placements. The first was with a family member and the next two were in foster homes which both said they would take the older brother but not Caleb due to his extreme behavioral issues.

When my husband and I met Caleb, we found him to be a very active child who lacked impulse control and the ability to regulate his emotions. Because of his unstable past, Caleb also found it a challenge to adjust to daily routines; for example, eating a snack at snack time, eating three balanced meals a day, and sleeping through the night.

The lack of stability in Caleb's life and not knowing if/when he would be moved next, made school a challenge for him. His teacher would say that Caleb could not stay in his seat, follow simple two-step directions, or walk quietly in the hall. When it came to school work, Caleb could not complete assignments without a teacher working one-on-one with him. When work was completed, it was rushed, sloppy, and incorrect. He had not retained the basic skills he had learned in kindergarten and first grade. Not only was Caleb behind academically but also cognitively.

The relationships with his peers also suffered. Caleb was awkward and did not know how to interact with others. He found it a challenge to keep his hands to himself. When he spoke to his classmates, his language was often harsh or inappropriate.

During class, Caleb was nicknamed the "Class Clown" because of his unpredictable outbursts and gestures in an attempt to be noticed or appreciated. While other classmates looked forward to recess, Caleb had to stay inside to complete his missed assignments. On days when he could go outside, he would lean against the building and cry because no one wanted to be his friend.

Another obstacle that influenced Caleb's behavior or ability to focus during school hours was "flashbacks" or resorting to earlier coping mechanisms without even realizing it. Simple, everyday situations would trigger memories from his past which caused him to go into a daze or react instinctually. Sometimes this would mean being overly sensitive to a loud or sudden noise causing him to cry or look for cover. Or perhaps it meant eating food from off of the floor or from a trashcan for fear that he would miss his next meal.

All of these different factors coupled together caused school to be one of Caleb's most stressful places, but with open communication between us, his teacher, school counselor, and the principal we were able to make progress. Some days were harder than others but when we took the time to step back and think about how far Caleb had come in just a month or two, or perhaps a quarter or semester, the teamwork was 100 percent worth it. My husband and I have learned that it takes a lot of love, consistency, and a willingness by all parties to try new approaches and strategies in order to help Caleb be successful at school. As foster parents, we have had to think long and hard about our definition of success. For Caleb, it meant making school a more pleasant experience and helping him learn the skills needed in order to retain the information and become a contributing member of his classroom.

MARTHA AND WILLIAM, FOSTER PARENTS OF 4 YEARS

Foster parenting is a difficult job. It may just be the hardest work an adult ever does. Foster parents will often find themselves exhausted, both mentally and physically, and feel drained. There is very little money available to help them, and they are sometimes not reimbursed for all the money spent on the foster child. The job will require these caregivers to work 24 hours a day, seven days a week, with no time off. Foster parents will sometimes feel overworked and underappreciated. These trained caregivers will work with children who are most likely coming from difficult and harmful environments. Some of these children will have health issues, some will come with behavioral issues, and some will struggle with learning disabilities. Many times, the children they work with will try their patience, and leave them with headaches, frustrations, disappointments, and even heartbreaks. There is a reason why many people are not foster parents, as it is often too difficult.

Yet, foster parents are truly making a tremendous difference in the lives of children in need. Though they may feel exhausted at times, and though they may feel that they are not making an impact, foster parents are changing the life of a child. Indeed, foster parents may know these children in need better than anyone else. They have wiped away their tears when the children cry at night from loneliness; taken them to the doctor with various medical needs; taught them important living and social skills that had been neglected; and watched over them as they struggled with the challenges and difficulties they face as a foster child.

In order for a child in foster care to succeed in school, his or her foster parents must be leading the charge and blazing a path as his advocate, fighting for the child's every chance. In truth, it is likely that the foster student will have no other person fighting for them, as the social worker's workload is an overwhelming one, and their teachers may be too busy to reach out with information, or may not have the necessary information about the child that they need in order to meet their needs. Therefore, it is up to the foster parent to be proactive in the child's life at school.

For many children in foster care, however, their foster parents are not very involved, as we explored in Chapter 5. Unfortunately, this will be to the detriment and disadvantage of the child. Instead, foster parents need to become as involved as possible with their foster child's school. The more a foster parent is seen in the school, the more the foster parent is heard by the teachers, the more the foster parent is involved in extra-curricular activities that the school offers for students, the more likely the child will succeed in school and later in life.

To begin with, foster parents need to ensure, from the very beginning when the child is placed into their home, that the child is enrolled in and attending school. As we have noted before, this may not always be the case for a child in care. Perhaps the child was never enrolled by their birth parents for that year; perhaps they are moving from one school district to another; perhaps they had been absent from school for great periods of time, and were not attending on a regular basis. In any case, foster parents need to make certain that their foster child is enrolled in school. Yet, before taking steps into their own hands, foster parents need to work alongside their foster child's social worker in this regard. After all, it is likely that the social worker is also working along the same line, and making plans to have the child enrolled. On the other hand, there is also the possibility that the child's social worker has many other responsibilities and tasks to attend to at that time, and may not be able to attend to enrollment right away. However, as we have examined throughout the preceding chapters, the more school a foster child misses, the further they will fall behind.

If the foster student should not have their transcripts and school records with them upon placement into a new foster home, foster parents should contact the child's social worker, asking this social worker about these important school documents. If indeed the social worker is too busy to attend to this at the time, foster parents should take steps to contact the previous school about the transcripts and school records. Perhaps, if need be and if possible, the foster parents can drive to the child's previous school and request the student's school documents. If a foster parent should do this, it is imperative that they have personal identification with them, as well as documentation that they have custody of the foster child. This may include signed papers by both the foster parents and the child's social worker. Schools will not release any school transcripts and records without this proof of custody. As a result, the child may not be able to enroll into their new school, and may even be classified as a "drop-out" if he or she should miss too many days.

In Chapter 5, we saw that many times teachers are unable to best assist a student in foster care, simply because they do not have enough information on the child, or any information for that matter. We also know that teachers do need this information if they are to be successful in meeting a foster child's specific needs and challenges. Foster parents can help teachers in this regard by sharing as much information as they are permitted to with school educators. Though there may be in place certain privacy laws and regulations in regard to sharing personal information with educators about students in foster care, the United States Congress passed the Uninterrupted Scholars Act, which amends the Family Educational Rights and Privacy Act (FERPA), to provide clarity about what is permissible in the sharing of education records with child welfare agencies. This will allow schools to release the child's education records to child welfare agencies without the prior written consent of the biological parents. The Uninterrupted Scholars Act is intended to improve the foster student's wellbeing, and to increase permanency within their foster home. This will be most helpful for foster parents when trying to obtain school records and transcripts for the student in care.

After obtaining transcripts and other school records, foster parents can be very helpful by delivering these to the student's new school. Furthermore, foster parents can also assist both the child and school educators by requesting to meet with the school teachers and counselor upon enrolling the student. During these meetings, foster parents can share with the school educators as much personal information as they are able and permitted to in regard to the child and their history, as well as any behavioral challenges and learning disabilities the child may be experiencing. If the foster parents are aware of any behavior modifications that might work for the child, these can be shared, as well. This information will go a long way for educators toward understanding the child, building positive relationships between the two, and helping the child succeed in the school.

Foster parents can also aid their foster child by reaching out to school employees, forming a positive and healthy working relationship with them. The child's foster parents should let school counselors, teachers, and administrators know that they can call the foster parents if needed, providing contact information to the educators, such as phone numbers and email addresses. Similarly, foster parents should obtain contact information from the child's teachers. Foster parents should attempt to remain in regular contact with the child's teachers. One way to do this is by requesting regular email updates from teachers and staff. Indeed, foster parents should use as many means of communication as possible. Through text messages, email, cell phones, Facebook, Twitter, and other social media platforms, there are numerous ways to be in contact with teachers and school employees. Foster parents can find out which one the teacher prefers, and use it to reach out to the child's educators. This may mean learning how to use these communication formats. Talk to others, take personal classes, and research how to use these various twenty-first century means of communication. After all, most teachers are busy, and a postal letter or landline phone call may not be the best means of staying in contact with the child's teachers and school counselor.

Along with this, teachers can ask the school counselor to set up a weekly progress report. In this report, teachers document the child's weekly grades, what assignments might be missing, upcoming tests, projects, and homework for the following week, and any behavior problems that might have occurred throughout the week. This weekly progress report could also include academic and behavioral successes the student exhibited during the week, allowing both teacher and foster parent the opportunity to praise the child in foster care, thus encouraging them to continue in this manner, building pride in their accomplishments, and knowledge that their efforts are recognized and appreciated. For many children in foster care, words of encouragement and praise are likely to have been seldom heard before coming into care, and can go a long way toward healing.

Not only should foster parents request regular behavior updates from the child's school, a responsible foster parent will also provide such information to the school. If a foster child should be having a particularly difficult time in the foster home, foster parents should let the teachers and counselors know, allowing these educators to be better prepared and equipped to handle any difficulties that might come their way. In Chapter 1, we saw that there are times when visitations with birth parents and biological family members may be distressing to a child, causing further emotional anxieties and concerns for the child; both leading up to the visitation and following it. These anxieties may spill over into the classroom, as the foster child struggles to manage the emotions that are spinning within him or her. As a result, the student may have a difficult time focusing on their school work, and their behavior, as they attempt to simply endure their feelings, and their status as a foster child.

When foster children are indeed having a difficult time with visitations, or are highly anxious about them, foster parents can help their child by informing the teachers beforehand. A note in the child's school agenda, an email, a text message, or a phone call; all are means that the foster parent can use to notify teachers and school counselors. Along with this, foster parents might suggest to the child's social worker that visitations and medical appointments be made after school, or on weekends, in order not to miss any more days of school, consequently falling even further behind. Though this recommendation may not be met by the social worker, it is important, nevertheless, for the foster parent to make this request, as it might just be granted.

Gary was a nine-year-old foster boy, and had been placed into his foster home due to abuse and neglect from his biological parents, who were eventually arrested for manufacturing and distributing illegal drugs from their home. During the first six months Gary was placed into his foster home, the child's parents were separated, while both awaited their time before the court to face the charges against them. The mother moved from home to home, staying with friends for short periods of time, while the father moved in with his own parents. Gary was a year behind in school, repeating the second grade, as he was greatly behind due to high levels of absenteeism. Gary's new foster parents were very devoted to their foster child's school, and spent much time helping the troubled child with his reading and writing skills.

The foster parents noticed that Gary would become anxious the morning of the visitation with his mother at the county's child welfare system's local office, as the young boy would become nervous about seeing her. Furthermore, Gary was coming home from school that day with reports from his teacher that he was not focused on his school work. Along with this, he was also displaying behavioral problems in his class on these days, with notes from his teacher that he would "act out." To further complicate things,

Gary would be so upset upon returning home from the visitations each week that he would have a very difficult time focusing on any of his homework, spelling words, and reading. Soon, Gary's foster parents came to realize that little to no homework could be accomplished that evening, and that the day at school, in general, would be one that was filled with anxiety and difficulty on the child's part. Hoping to improve the situation for all involved, and make it easier for both his teacher and themselves, Gary's foster parents requested a conference with his second grade teacher.

When they met, the foster parents notified Gary's teacher about what they were observing each week before and after Gary's visitation with his mother, and revealing to the child's teacher the reasoning behind the child's behavioral issues that were related to it. It was during this time that the foster parents asked their foster child's teacher if she would be more lenient on assigning homework on the evenings that visitations took place, allowing for additional time to accomplish the work. As the mother's housing situation was one that was not stable, her visitation schedule was not a consistent or regular one, and the foster parents were often not notified until the day before by the child's social worker. As a result, Gary's foster parents conveyed that they would inform the student's teacher each time a visitation took place with a short note placed into the child's book bag, as well as an email.

Many children in foster care will be coming from environments and homes where school was not a focus, nor was education stressed as much of a concern. Foster parents need to be both prepared for this, and compassionate for it, in what could be a difficult time after school each day. The foster child may not be used to doing homework, may have a difficult time being focused upon it, may suffer from learning disabilities, or may simply resist spending time doing work after school. Indeed, he or she may experience feelings of frustration if they are behind in their school work and learning. One of the keys to success between the foster child and foster parent regarding homework is to set reasonable and realistic expectations for the child. Foster parents need to find out where the child's learning ability and level of knowledge is at, and work with the child at this level. Talk to the child's teachers about the child's abilities, and whether any accommodations need to be made. This is not to say that foster parents should not motivate the child to succeed at a higher level. Indeed, foster parents should encourage their foster child to set goals and expectations, as these caregivers may be the only adults who have ever given the child any confidence and encouragement in school. Nevertheless, foster parents should not push a child beyond his or her abilities, as it will only frustrate all involved even more so. Instead, talk to them about what success means for the child, and help them to set goals for themselves. Celebrate every success, no matter how small it may be.

Foster children will likely have a difficult time concentrating on their homework, as they instead focus on simply wanting to go home, and the many emotional distractions that come with being a foster child. To help the child with homework time, foster parents can prepare a quiet area for them to do their work, if possible. It should be a place that is away from distractions, such as television, video games, and other media that may interrupt their concentration. Perhaps consider setting up an "office" for the older students, complete with desk, materials, and even a bulletin board with lists of upcoming projects and school due dates. This office might be in the corner of the kitchen, living room, or their own bedroom. Foster parents might even stop phone calls during this time, as well. Set up a regular time each day for the child to do their homework, so they will know what to expect when they come home from school. If the adults in the house have projects to work on, or books to read, they may wish to do so during this time, and in view of the child, so that the student sees that homework and reading is a normal part of life, setting the correct atmosphere for the child.

When it is time for the foster student to begin their homework, foster parents should review with them what the child is to work on. Go over the assignments with the child, ensuring that he or she understands what needs to be done, that the directions are clear, and what is expected of them. Ask if the child has any questions, and provide assistance if necessary. As many children in foster care struggle with their reading and math skills, the child may need the foster parents' help with studying for tests, reading aloud, and other school tasks. If the student has work in several different subjects, help them to organize and prioritize what needs to be done. When there are days when they have no homework, encourage the child to read a book of their choice, either aloud to you or by themselves. Foster children, like all children, can never read enough, and many have never had an adult or parent that they could read to. If the child is young, the foster parent can read a book to them, and try to do so daily, as many children in foster care are behind in their reading skills.

Help the student to set short-term and long-term goals. Perhaps consider creating a reward system for them. For those children in foster care who are younger, a colorful chart or poster can be created, in which the days of the week are represented, and the homework they have for each class and each day. When one assignment is completed, the foster parent can place a sticker on the chart, measuring progress. For those foster students who are older, they could be rewarded for accomplishing their homework and their goals with a later weekend bedtime or curfew, more television time, or some other incentive that they might appreciate. It might also be wise to allow the student to have breaks if there is a lot of school work to be accomplished in one afternoon. When the foster child is finished with all homework and projects, teach them how to place it into a separate folder, one that is used for work to be turned in, and remind the student each morning to turn in all work.

For those foster students who have learning disabilities and challenges, a world of educational resources is available to them. From books and resources in public and school libraries, to countless websites and resources found online, as well as those that can be provided by the teachers and educators at the foster child's school, there is something available for every learning disability, including songs, games, study tips, products, behavior management tips, and much more. A list of some of these online resources and websites can be found in the Resources section, at the conclusion of this book. After finding out what unique learning challenges their foster child faces, foster parents should seek out and locate the appropriate academic and educational resources.

The development and use of appropriate and healthy social skills is another way foster parents can help their children. Certainly, these are important skills that the children will need, not only in school and in their foster home, but in the future, especially for those foster children who age out of the system. These skills will be relied upon when they seek a job, a place to live, or assistance in some way. Along with this, positive social skills will also help foster children to withstand difficult times, and if they are rejected by their peers, and even those who are supposed to love them the most. While some children prefer higher levels of social interaction and others prefer less, all children in care will need their foster parents to help guide them in developing these important skills.

There are a number of ways that foster parents can help their foster student regarding his or her social skills. To begin with, it is important for foster parents to remember that they themselves are the role model, and that the foster child will learn the most from simply watching and observing how their foster parents interact with others. Instead of telling the child how to act in certain ways, the foster parents also need to teach the child social skills, and then model those skills themselves throughout their daily tasks and lives. Let us not forget that foster children will be silently watching their foster parents in all they say and do, and that foster parents are often the best role model the child may have ever had in their life.

As with academic studies and behavior in school, foster parents also need to set realistic expectations with their foster child in the area of social skills. Remembering that many children in foster care came from homes where they were not taught these basic social skills, foster parents need to be patient in helping the child develop these skills. Indeed, it may take quite some time, and at times it may seem that the child might never learn these skills. Yet, patience and understanding by the foster parent in this is crucial if the child is to better adjust socially in the school setting, and later in life.

Along with this, foster parents should teach their foster student the importance of using good manners at all times, saying "Please" and "Thank you" to others, words that might be foreign to the child's previous home environment. The student may not appreciate the importance of using only positive words toward others, possibly having been raised in a home where negative words, insults, and verbal abuse were the norm. Foster parents may need to teach the child the timeless adage, "If you have nothing nice to say, don't say anything at all." Demonstrate the importance of having and showing respect for all others. Instruct the child how to make and maintain eye contact with others during a conversation, including with teachers and fellow students. Help the child learn how to focus on paying attention to conversations, and not letting their mind wander off. Along with this is the value of knowing how to begin and end appropriate conversations, and the significance of not monopolizing an entire conversation, nor of interrupting when another is talking.

The importance of personal space, and learning how to not invade it, is another skill that may be lacking with the child. The child may also need to be taught how to manage and control their emotions, and the simple art of counting to ten when they are feeling anger or frustration, or being provoked by others. The child may also need to be shown the importance of being patient with others, another trait they might not have experienced in their previous home. Encourage the child to also express his or her feelings to others, instead of containing them within so that they build up inside until they release in a negative and harmful fashion. Finally, help the child to develop skills regarding problem solving, and how to effectively confront challenging situations in a healthy and positive way.

Foster parents can also help their foster student in the development of these skills by encouraging the child to participate in activities outside the classroom. Many schools have extra-curricular organizations, and activities with various school sports, music, and clubs. Likewise, community sports and organizations also allow the child the opportunity to not only participate and develop these skills, but to learn new skills, develop talents, and to exercise. Again, it is important to remember that many of these social skills were likely not taught to the child, nor valued in the child's previous home, and that they will take time to develop. Volunteering in school activities is another method that foster parents can use when attempting to help their child in school. Volunteering in the child's school does not need to be extensive, as foster parents can volunteer their time for as much or as little as they like in many schools. Studies have shown that those children who have parents who volunteer generally earn better grades, score higher on tests, show better social skills, and have improved behavior (Lewis, Kim, and Bey 2011).

As we examined in Chapter 4, there are many perils and pitfalls for those teens who age out of the foster care system. Since many foster children do not graduate from high school, they find it difficult to obtain a job that will be able to provide for them financially. Adding to this, most simply do not have the skills, training, or tools necessary for procuring a stable job. Many foster children who age out also turn to drugs and even crime, thus resulting in jail sentences. Indeed, the percentage of those in jail at any given time in the United States who have had some experience with foster care in their lives is well over 70 percent. Certainly, it is a bleak future that most foster children face as they age out of a system; a system that may have failed them with the resources, training, and support they sorely need in order to be a success, or even a positive contribution to society. Many foster students are either not aware of these grim realities, or not appreciative of how much they might be at risk of becoming one of these disturbing statistics.

Foster parents can help to prevent many of these problems from arising in the first place by attending to some tasks while a child is in their care. As soon as a foster child is ready, foster parents should begin teaching the child the fundamentals of personal financial responsibility by helping to develop simple money skills. Help the child by opening up and managing a personal bank account, as well as teaching them how to balance a budget. Allow a foster child to learn how to cook. Teach the child how to clean and take care of a household and general first aid. Practice filling out job and college applications. Perhaps most importantly, foster parents should stress the importance of education and encourage the child to graduate from high school.

Perhaps the biggest impact one can make with those who have aged out of the system is to become an advocate of change.

By contacting lawmakers, politicians, and publicity agents through means of emails, letters, phone calls, and other means of communication, one can bring attention to the needs of these young adults who are facing a series of challenges after leaving the foster care system. Along with this, these advocates of change can also post information in editorial letters, websites, public forums, and so forth. By lobbying for change, new laws can be introduced, and information can be brought forward to the general public.

Indeed, there are many ways a foster parent can help their students in foster care succeed in school. As we have seen, without the support of the foster parent, children in care are likely to struggle, and may even fail in both academic studies and behavior. For the child to not only to do well, but to succeed in these areas, they will need their foster parents to be included, invested, and involved.

CHAPTER 9

How Social Workers Can Help

Children in foster care lack two very important characteristics in their lives: consistency and stability. As these children are moved from their birth homes into one foster home after another, and from one school after another, the lack of a consistent supportive and caring adult in their lives is a traumatic one. Indeed, the lack of stability in their lives can result in the inability to create healthy attachments with others, to develop positive social skills, and to trust others. Along with this, as a foster student is moved from one school to the next on a frequent basis, they will likely fall behind academically, as we have examined throughout this book. For these children in care, their social worker may be the only stable and consistent person in their lives. Indeed, social workers may be the only adults who are able to ensure that all of their educational needs are met, as the child moves from placement to placement.

To that end, social workers must become involved in a foster child's education on a regular basis, making this one of their chief focuses regarding the child. Without a doubt, the protection and safety of the child is paramount; yet the child's education is a large key to his or her future success in life. In some cases, a foster child's social worker may delegate responsibility for the student's education to the foster parent, or perhaps even to a court-appointed special advocate (CASA) that has been assigned to the child. Yet, the ultimate responsibility of the child's education lies with the social worker, who is to ensure that all of the child's needs are met, including their education.

Perhaps the best way a social worker can help a foster child with their education is by attempting to place them in a home that is within the same school district, whenever possible. If there are foster parents living in the same school district as the student in care who are able to have the child placed into their own home, social workers should strive to see that this is accomplished. While this may not be achievable every time, it is highly recommended if the potential is there. After all, as we have seen, each time a child is displaced into another school, the trauma only increases for them, in several ways. Some of these traumas can be reduced if the foster child remains in their own school during this time of transition. Familiar faces, consistent teachers, friends and classmates, and the same classes can help to alleviate the trauma that is associated with being taken from the child's biological family members and placed into a foster home. Along with this, there will not be the large amounts of absenteeism that are associated with moving from one school to the next.

Often, social workers do not have the option, or the ability, to place a child into a foster home that lies within their original school district. When a child is moved into a new school, social workers should strive to have the child enrolled within three days of placement into their new foster home. This will help prevent the attendance problems that often plague children in foster care, thus causing them to fall behind with their academic studies. As examined in this book, children in care are often without their school transcripts and records when moved from one school to another. Social workers should retrieve these documents from the child's previous school, and provide them to the child's new school, as soon as possible. Furthermore, social workers should keep an up-to-date record of all grades and school information for their own files on the child, including report cards, progress reports, behavior reports, and other information pertinent to the student's school status, thus gathering all educational documentation on the child for their case file. This will assist in future planning for the child, as well as be a source of information if the child should be moved to another school, another foster home, or even to another social worker.

Along with this information, social workers should request to meet with the school's counselor, and deliver any concerns in regard to the foster student. Furthermore, social workers can request to work alongside the school counselor when developing the foster student's class schedule and placement. Social workers should also form a working relationship with the school system's psychologists in order to maximize the child's success and identify problems early. This can be a most important relationship for the success of the child, in regard to both their academic studies and behavior. As social workers are likely to know more about the child and their needs than anyone else, they will be invaluable to the child's progress in school, as well as to his or her placement into classes.

Social workers should request to work alongside school employees, as together they work to plan which classes and courses would best meet the needs of the foster child. Indeed, the student's social worker should be heavily engaged in the child's academic planning, as well as in any and all educational decision making. This is especially significant, as school officials will not have the necessary information they need in order to meet the needs of the child, and may place them in the wrong classroom and wrong courses as a result. Foster care social workers need to make sure that the student is referred to the appropriate learning programs that would be of benefit to them. If the child needs to be tested for special programs, the social worker should advocate for these. In order to be fully aware of any and all programs and services that can be of an advantage for the foster student, social workers need to be up-to-date and familiar with the educational services foster children are entitled to under federal and state laws, and make certain that the child is offered them. If these educational services are not being provided, the social worker should notify the child's attorney.

Moreover, social workers should attempt to attend any planning meeting that involves the child, including Individual Education Plans (IEPs). During these meetings and planning events, social workers should be vocal and involved, ensuring that their voice, and in effect the voice of the student, is heard. As noted in Chapter 5, teachers and school employees have not been trained in the unique challenges that children in foster care face. In addition, schools often do not also have the resources they need to best assist foster students. Social workers can provide resources, such as training books and manuals, that help in better understanding these challenges. The more that school employees better understand these needs, the more they are likely to be flexible in helping the child as he or she struggles.

Teachers and school employees may be too busy to contact both the foster parents and the social workers if problems should arise, as we noted in Chapter 5. There may be times when social workers need to be notified, yet are not. Failure to turn in school work, poor grades, lack of attendance, and poor behavior are all instances where social workers need to be informed and advised. Regular and consistent contact between the social workers and school educators is essential. Social workers need to put this into action themselves, instead of waiting for communication from the school; communication that may come too late, or never at all. Through phone calls, emails, texting, and other online methods, social workers have the ability to stay in touch with a foster child's teachers like never before. Not only can social workers request information, grade updates, and behavior status from school employees, but they can also help teachers by reciprocating with information of their own. Social workers should notify teachers and school counselors in advance of any visitations between student and biological family members, court appearances, and other dates when the child will be absent from the classroom.

Along with this, teachers should also be notified from the social worker during those times when the child in foster care is exhibiting behavior problems, perhaps due to these visitations and court appearances. It may be that those visitations or court appearances are particularly stressful and traumatic for the child. Indeed, many times children in care return to their foster homes with feelings of grief, loss, sorrow, rejection, disappointment, and other emotions of anguish. As a result, it can be most difficult for them to concentrate their attention toward school assignments and studying. Furthermore, they may have difficulty focusing in the classroom, as they struggle trying to just manage their own emotions and behavior. When these court appearances and visitations do occur, social workers can request that accommodations be made with homework, test dates, school projects, and behavior incidents that fall around those times. As we have noted before, teachers are often willing to be more flexible and compassionate toward the foster child in regard to both assigning homework and discipline when they understand the nature of the child's behavior.

As social workers are most likely to best know the child, their needs, and the challenges that confront them in all areas of their life, these social workers should also educate themselves on the potential barriers that the student might face while in school. With a better understanding of any obstacles that might come the child's way, these pitfalls that they might encounter while in school can be minimized. These barriers may include lost books, eye glasses and vision problems, loss of hearing and hearing aids, difficulties with transportation to school and to school events, unpaid fees and charges, and language barriers and the need for an interpreter for the child. All these barriers are an obstruction to the student's learning and education, and they will need their social worker to help overcome these obstacles.

The social worker should also strive to visit the child while in school. Perhaps stop by and have lunch with the child; attend a program they are involved in, such as music, sports, or art; or simply observe them during a class period. If the child is not involved in extra-curricular activities, such as sports and fine arts, social workers can encourage the student to participate. The act of participation can go toward helping the child with their social skills. The simple appearance of the social worker in the school and at after-school programs may reinforce to the child that they are cared for, and that someone has their best interests at heart. After all, a supportive word often goes far.

Without a doubt, the working relationship between a foster child's social worker and the child's teachers is important. However, just as important is the working relationship between the social worker and the student's foster parents. If the child placed into foster care is to succeed in school, adjust to their foster home, and begin to heal from the traumas that plague them, there must be a positive and healthy working relationship between these two groups. Therefore, social workers need to be proactive in both seeking out this relationship and developing it, ensuring that it is a positive and effective one. If the foster parents are not involved in the child's school, social workers can encourage them to become more active. They should provide information on why this is important, and how it will benefit the foster student, in all areas. Social workers should also see to it that foster parents they work with are engaged with the child's teachers, and in regular communication with them. If these foster parents do not have the correct contact information, including email addresses, phone numbers, and so on, social workers should provide these. Further, the social workers should set up a time for teachers and foster parents to meet, if they have not done so already. Along with this, social workers should see that foster parents are receiving information from the schools about their foster child's grades and report cards, behavior status, resources, and all other information regarding the student and their school. Finally, foster parents should be enthusiastically encouraged by their child's social worker to become active and strong advocates for the child.

By working alongside the foster student, social workers can help the child to be successful in their education in a variety of ways. First, social workers should sit down with the child, and explain to them the importance of school, their grades, and their behavior. Speaking to the child in terms, words, and phrases that they can understand, social workers should stress the importance to the child that they should do their best, no matter what school they attend, and no matter who their teachers might be. Listen to their concerns and fears with a compassionate and understanding ear, asking the child how they might be able to best address these, allowing them to offer suggestions on their own. If they have no suggestions, discuss with them possible solutions to any problems they might be facing in school. Additionally, social workers should try to engage the child in his or her academic planning, trying to include them in any way possible in their education decision making. By allowing the child some input into the decision making, they may feel more persuaded to do their best, in regard to both academic studies and behavior.

There is no doubt that social workers are very busy. Yet, if time permits during a visit with the foster child, they can also spend a few moments listening to the child read. Certainly, many young children like to be listened to as they read a book aloud. After all, another listening and patient adult will be a positive influence for the child. If the child is struggling in some areas in school, or needs some help with homework, spend a few moments and try to assist them with it, if possible. Help them find the resources they might need that will support them with their school work. Encourage them to become more socially active in school by making new friends, trying out for sports, and participating in fine arts and school organizations.

For many children in foster care, education has never been stressed as important by those they may have lived with, and graduation from high school never seen as a goal that they should obtain. Social workers should stress the importance of not only performing to the best of their ability in school, but to graduate, and not drop out when difficulties arise. Indeed, the importance of obtaining a high school diploma should be stressed in a consistent and unfailing manner, and social workers should make every effort to see that this becomes a reality for the foster student.

Social workers can also support children in care by helping them plan for their future after post-secondary education, or after high school. If the foster teen has the academic ability to attend college, the social worker can help the student by looking at college options. Visit universities with them, and help them fill out applications. Help them examine other options besides college, including that of the military. If the child should choose to age out of the system, they will need skills that can help them later in life. As many aged-out foster youth cannot afford school, assistance in this manner is most helpful. Communities can begin a foster scholarship fund, setting up a college fund for those foster children wishing to further their education. Supplies for school can be donated to local foster care agencies who work with children who will soon age out, as described in Chapter 7.

There are times when a foster student will be returned to their home, and back to their original school. Indeed, there are several reasons why a foster child might be removed from a foster home. Over 50 percent of foster children are reunited with their parents, while roughly 10 percent will go to live with other members of the biological family, such as aunts and uncles and grandparents. Eighteen percent of foster children will end up being adopted, as well. When a child is returned to their home and family members, or adopted by another family, it is important that the social worker provides all educational information to the family the child is moving to. Social workers should help the family in preparing for this educational transition. Sit down with the family and share with them the child's academic status and needs, any concerns regarding their behavior, and any and all resources they are currently using or will need to use. Communicate with them in an enthusiastic way any and all positive steps and progress the child made while in their foster home and school, in respect to both grades and behavior. If the child is involved in any sports or other school activities and organizations, try to persuade the family and the child to continue with these at the new school, as this will help make it easier in yet another transition to yet another school.

The return to the child's original school will be yet another transition. After all, the foster child is leaving another school, where they may have formed positive and healthy relationships with the teachers, school educators, and fellow students. The return to their original school may not be as smooth a transition as many might think. The longer the child has been away from their initial school, and the greater the passage of time, the more likely it is that they will return to a school that is different, with different faces and different teachers, as some of the child's friends and former teachers may have moved on during their time away. Indeed, the child may experience feelings of grief and loss while returning back to their biological family members, as he or she misses their foster family, new friends, and teachers, as well as those who have moved from their previous school. As a result, the student may struggle in their former school, with both academic studies and behavior. Thus, social workers should encourage the biological family members to become involved in the school, and to be prepared for any challenges and difficulties the child may face; whether it is with the emotions faced as the child returns home, or with the challenges they face with their academic studies and learning disabilities. Along with this, the social worker should stress that the biological family members help the child maintain expectations of academic success and proper behavior while in school. Moreover, biological family members should be encouraged by the social worker to help the child in regard to keeping the child's school working environment a consistent one; helping them with their homework, reading along with them, and assisting them with studying.

Furthermore, social workers should meet with educators at the child's original school to ensure that he or she is placed into the appropriate classes. Since coming into foster care, it is likely that the foster student has been placed into the appropriate classes and received the appropriate support that they need academically; classes and support they may not have received when originally enrolled in the original school. It will be essential for the child's continued success that they do receive the resources and support, and be placed in the appropriate classroom and courses, and the social worker should strive to make certain that this is the case. Additionally, it will be quite helpful if the social worker meets with the teachers of the foster student and shares with them as much information about the child as possible. Even though the child may be returning to some of their original classes, the child's former teachers, administrators, and school counselor may not be familiar with any changes or advancements the child has made since moving to another school. The information regarding these changes and advances is important for teachers and school educators in order to best meet the needs of the student, and to help them continue with any progress they may have made while placed in foster care.

For a child in foster care, a social worker may be the most consistent and stable person in their life. This consistency will be most important as they move from home to home, and school to school. Social workers might be the lifeline, or life raft, the child needs to hold onto as he or she tries to survive the tumultuous waves that threaten to overtake them in school and in their turbulent life. The social worker will be the lighthouse during those trying and dark times the child faces in school. The advocacy and support the social worker provides for the child is crucial for the foster student's survival in our schools today.

CHAPTER 10

Creating a Support Team

Attending school can be a massive struggle for a child who lives in foster care. These children already have so many strikes against them, just by the nature of their experiences. They have suffered environmental deprivation, abuses of varying types, nutritional and emotional neglect, and any number of losses and terrifying experiences. These children often have deficits in learning that are the result of prenatal trauma, educational neglect, or sporadic school attendance. Their world may have been such a scary place that they have chronically high adrenaline and cortisol levels making them hypervigilant and always on the lookout for danger. They may also have sensory integration or processing disorders that make the world seem a strange, loud, disorderly, painful, or frightening place! Entering into the foster care system is categorically terrifying for these children who, despite being pulled from a bad situation into one that should be safe, enriching, and healing, only want to go back to the "devil they know" and have innate fears of what they are being thrust into. They almost always have to go to a new school, which is frightening for a child from the healthiest family; imagine what it must be for a child who has suffered as our children in foster care have!

Cheryl was 13 years old when she came into foster care. She had suffered from a chaotic lifestyle and was the "black sheep" of her very dysfunctional family. Cheryl's mother had severe intellectual and developmental disabilities and her father was very controlling and rigid, limiting his daughters' contact with people outside the family. This rigid, enmeshed family dynamic creates an environment that is ripe for abuse. Cheryl became the family workhorse; responsible for all chores and maintenance of the house as well as caring for her mother's physical and hygiene needs. Her older and more beautiful sister was elevated to the role of her father's mistress and female head of the household. Cheryl's sense of self-worth suffered mightily in this setting.

In addition, her education was sorely neglected and she entered the foster care system with extensive learning disabilities and several years behind in school.

The 13-year-old foster child had the good fortune to be placed with a very loving older foster couple. This couple was our "go-to" family for children with special needs. They saw the beauty and preciousness inside every child and were able to look past external characteristics to know what was inside. More importantly, they knew how to work with children to bring that lovely inside to the outside! Cheryl very quickly felt safe and accepted in this foster family and she began to grow and blossom at home. At school, on the other hand, Cheryl continued to struggle. She did not believe that she could ever succeed in school and, what's more, she saw no reason to do so. She couldn't imagine herself employed or doing much of anything except house chores and maybe meeting a boy who would like her.

Cheryl was in special education classes and the school staff were working hard to help her to catch up on all she had missed. She had modifications in all of her classes, but even with these, she consistently brought homework grades home that were in the range of 5 to 15 points out of 100! Well, one day Cheryl brought home one piece of homework that had a grade of 20 on it! Now, for most children, a score of 20 percent is nothing to write the papers about, but for Cheryl it was an improvement of between 33 and 75 percent! Now that's a big deal and this very wise foster mama knew it and knew she had to capitalize on this accomplishment! Mrs. Johnson took that paper and, after hugging and praising Cheryl and telling everyone in the house what a red letter day it was for her, she stuck it to the refrigerator with a magnet and circled that score of 20 with a red marker. From that day forward, every single person who came to the house got dragged to the refrigerator and Cheryl got to tell how she worked so hard to get that grade while Mrs. Johnson beamed at her, patted her on the back, and told each and every person how proud she was of Cheryl's accomplishment.

As you might imagine, grades around 20 percent started to be more common for Cheryl and before long she brought home a paper with a 25 on it. Well, here we went again! Hug and praise Cheryl—CHECK! Brag to the whole family—CHECK! Paper stuck to fridge—CHECK! Praise and recognition for a job well done in front of every visitor to the house—CHECK!

This activity progressed over the course of the school year and, as time went on, Cheryl's grades made it up to the passing range in all of her classes. Her reading and math levels improved, she started to show more interest in school, and she even started to care a little more about her personal appearance and hygiene. Eventually, Cheryl was able to graduate from high school and move on to have a productive life with some healthy relationships and personal success. All of this would not have happened without a foster mama who understood the need to meet this child right where she was in order to help her to move to a better place. Cheryl is an adult now and Mr. and Mrs. Johnson have both passed on. Cheryl maintains her relationship with Mrs. Johnson's adult birth daughter, several adopted children, and other children who were fortunate to be fostered in that home and who have all built their own little family on the foundations laid by Mr. and Mrs. Johnson!

GINNY J., SOCIAL WORKER OF 26 YEARS

Teamwork. In many areas of life, teamwork is essential in order to have success. Business, sports teams, non-profit companies, and other organizations all depend upon the concept of teamwork, with each doing their part in order to accomplish a goal. In order for a child in foster care to truly achieve success in school, let alone simply survive in it, they must have a group of people behind them, helping, encouraging, and advocating for them. Many times, for this child in foster care, this might be the first time they have ever had people teaming up to help them, coming together in support of them. A support team comprising teachers, foster parents, and social worker is essential to the academic and behavioral success for the foster student. When all three sets of stakeholders work together as a team, the child will surely benefit. As we have seen, each member of this team, each stakeholder, is important for the success of the child. If one is missing, the child will not have the full support they so very much need.

When creating a support team for the foster child, it will be helpful to begin by determining who will act as the "point person," or one who will help by coordinating. Normally, this point person, or coordinator, should be someone who is well organized and responsible. If possible, the student's foster parent is ideal to fill this role, as they will be the most familiar with the child at the current time, and the child's need, as well as the challenges that the foster child is facing at the time. As noted in Chapter 8, foster parents need to take the lead in advocating for their foster child, reaching out to teachers for their assistance. When the foster child is enrolled into the school, the child's foster parent should then begin the process of creating this support team by contacting the child's teachers and social worker, setting up a time to meet and a location that is agreeable to all. Most likely, the best location will be at the child's school, though it might also be the local child welfare office or even the public library. Wherever that location might be, seek permission first, explaining what the meeting will be held for, and who will be in attendance. Along with setting a location and time, ask that each team member of the support group bring any and all relevant information about the child that can be shared with others.

When the initial meeting is held, the point person should ensure that all participants are introduced, and that all feel welcome. After each participant signs a sign-in sheet, the coordinator should ask for a volunteer to record minutes of the meeting. After this, members of the support group should review all data and information about the child, sharing with each other information they have about the child, and any observations they might have made regarding the child that others on the team will find useful, as well as help them better understand the foster child.

Once a relationship has been formed between members of this team, it must be maintained and given constant attention in order for it to continue and prosper. Members can help to maintain it through the use of emails and internet forums, phone calls and phone chains, letters and mailing lists, and through the use of the evaluation form, which helps to assist the team in remaining focused on future meetings. Higher performing schools value a partnership with parents and members of the community. Schools need not only provide training to administrators and teachers regarding collaboration between parents and community members, they must also encourage members of the community, as well as parents, to volunteer within the school as well as contribute in other ways.

Communication is vital in order for a home–school–community partnership to work effectively. Schools must work more diligently at two-way communications between school

CREATING A SUPPORT TEAM

and community via newsletters, phone calls, emails, and a school website. Schools need to also embrace the newest technology in such communication modes as blogs, Skype, and other virtual media that favor meaningful parental involvement. A communicative relationship should already be created before the student begins the first day of class within the school, during teachers' pre-planning sessions. Teachers, social workers, and foster parents need to create a working team when creating lesson plans specifically for the foster child. Along with this, the team needs to communicate when making future plans for the child, as well as confer when important decisions in regard to the foster student's needs are made. Team members can also share resources that assist the foster student together. Community members and parents can also work alongside schools by assisting students with their homework, as well as keeping track of their academic progress. Also, parents and community members can attend school functions, student activities, and parent nights.

The foster parent, as point person, must be prepared for each meeting regarding the foster child. In the Appendix, there are some templates that might be of use. Indeed, these are templates I designed for my own use with several of my foster children when I met with their teachers and social workers.

Foster children often have a difficult time with exhibiting proper school behavior during the school day. For many of the children, school is a constant reminder that they are, indeed, foster children without a true home. The continuous reminder that their peers are living with biological family members while they are not is a difficult reality for them, and can be manifested in several ways. Some foster children simply withdraw and become antisocial, in an attempt to escape their current environment and world they have been thrust into. For many foster children, violent behavior becomes the norm, as they not only act out in a negative and disruptive fashion in the school, but in their foster home, too, prompting yet another move to another foster home and another school.

Schools are indeed a difficult environment for foster children, and, far too often, these foster children are unable to meet the demands and challenges that are placed upon them while enrolled in a school. It is only with the combined help of the foster parents, social worker, and teachers that a foster child has a chance at success. By working together, all members of these three groups will be better equipped to assist foster children as they grow older and contribute to the community and society in a positive way as a means of greater social change.

APPENDIX
New Foster Student Protocol and Team Meeting Materials

Social Workers/Foster Parents/ Teachers Checklist

Upon enrollment of a new foster student, the following tasks should be attended to meet the needs, as well as ease the transition.

Social worker:

- ❏ Provide transcripts and records to school

- ❏ Deliver information to school counselor and administrators about discipline/learning disabilities

- ❏ Establish and maintain regular contact with teachers

- ❏ Provide educational/emotional background information to teachers

- ❏ Assist foster parents in encouraging child with school work

- ❏ Update school on problems in regard to emotional struggles as well as from visitations with biological family members

- ❏ Encourage contact between foster parents and teachers

- ❏ Provide resource materials about foster care/foster children to teachers/counselors/administrators

- ❏ Attend school functions, such as sporting events and parent nights, that involve foster child

★

Foster parent:

- ❑ Reach out to teachers/school counselor/administrators and form working relationship/team

- ❑ Update emotional/behavioral/academic successes and failures to teachers

- ❑ Inform teachers and school counselors about visitation dates and times, and any problems that may result

- ❑ Assist foster child with homework and studying

- ❑ Attend school functions, such as sporting events and parent nights, that involve foster child

Teacher:

- ❑ Deliver all academic updates to foster parents and social workers

- ❑ Observe foster child for any unusual or troubling behavior

- ❑ Report any unusual behavior to foster parents and social workers

- ❑ Become proactive; develop a positive rapport with child through use of daily conversation

- ❑ Provide an active listening ear for the child

- ❑ Be a positive role model

- ❑ Respect the child

- ❑ Develop discipline that works for foster child with foster parents/social workers and use it in classroom setting

- ❑ Attend school functions, such as sporting events and parent nights, that involve foster child

★

Foster Student Support Team Meeting Evaluation Form

Name
Teacher
Social worker
Foster parent
Other

Next Meeting:

Date		Time	
Location			

★

Meeting Evaluation Form

Date: Time of Day:

Questions:

Comments:

Did the meeting start on time?

Were meeting objectives met?

Was the agenda followed?

Did the discussion remain focused?

Were participants adequately prepared?

★

Was the location appropriate?

Did the meeting end on time?

Has a follow-up report been sent?

Were ground rules adhered to?

Was everyone involved?

The strengths of the meeting were:

The meeting could have been improved by:

REFERENCES

The AFCARS Report (2009) Adoption and Foster Care Analysis and Reporting System [AFCARS] Available at www.acf.hhs.gov/sites/default/files/cb/afcarsreport20.pdf, accessed on 8 June 2015.

Altshuler (1997). "A reveille for school social workers: Children in foster care need our help!" Social Work, 19 (2), 121-127. Available at http://findarticles.com/p/articles/mi_hb6467/is_1_48/ai_n28976792/pg_9/, accessed on 8 June 2015.

American Academy of Pediatrics (2000) "Developmental issues for young children in foster care." *Pediatrics* 106, 5, 1145–1150.

Amster, B., Greis, S., and Silver, J. (1997) *Feeding and Language Disorders in Young Children in Foster Care.* Paper presented at the annual meeting of the Speech-Language Hearing Association, Boston.

Ayasse, R. (1995) "Addressing the needs of foster children: The foster youth services program." *Social Work in Education 17*, 4, 207–216.

Benedict, M.I., Zuravin, S., and Stallings, R.Y. (1996) "Adult functioning of children who lived in kin versus nonrelative family foster homes." *Child Welfare 77*, 529–549.

Berrick, J. D., Barth, R. P., and Needell, B. (1994) "A comparison of kinship foster homes and foster family homes: Implications for kinship foster care as family preservation." *Children and Youth Services Review 16*, 1/2, 35–63.

Bowlby, J. (1982). Attachment (2nd ed.). New York, NY: Basic Books.

California Department of Social Services (2002) *Report on the Survey of the Housing Needs of Emancipated Foster/Probation Youth.* Sacramento, CA: CDSS.

Calvin, E. (2001) *Make a Difference in a Child's Life: A Manual for Helping Children and Youth Get What They Need in School.* Seattle, WA: TeamChild and Casey Family Programs.

Canning, R. (1974) "School experiences of foster children." *Child Welfare 73*, 582–586.

Cantos, A., Gries, L., and Slis, V. (1997) "Behavioral correlates of parental visiting during family foster care." *Child Welfare 76*, 2, 309–329.

Chall, J.S. (1983) *Stages of Reading Development.* New York, NY: McGraw-Hill Book Company.

Child Welfare League of America (2005) *Quick Facts About Foster Care.* Available at: www.cwla.org/programs/fostercare/factsheet.htm, accessed on 8 June 2015.

Christian, S. (2003) *Educating Children in Foster Care.* Washington, DC: National Conference of State Legislatures.

Clausen, J., Landsverk, J., Ganger, W., Chadwick, D., and Litrownik, A. (1998) "Mental health problems of children in foster care." *Journal of Child and Family Studies 7*, 3, 283–296.

Coulling, N. (2000) "Definitions of successful education for the looked after child: A multi-agency perspective." *Support for Learning 15*, 1, 30–35.

Courtney, M., Piliavin, I., Grogan-Kaylor, A., and Nesmith, A. (2001) "Foster youth transitions to adulthood: A longitudinal view of youth leaving care." *Child Welfare League of America 80*, 6, 685–717.

Courtney, M. and Dworsky, A. (2005) *Midwest Evaluation of the Adult Functioning of Former Foster Youth.* Chicago: Chapin Hall Center for Children at the University of Chicago.

Courtney, M.E. and Heuring, D.H. (2005) "The Transition to Adulthood for Youth 'Aging Out' of the Foster Care System." In D.W. Osgood, E.M. Foster, C. Flanagan, and G.R. Ruth (eds) *On Your Own Without a Net: The Transition to Adulthood for Vulnerable Populations.* Chicago: University of Chicago Press.

Davey, D. and Pithouse, A. (2008) "Schooling and looked after children: Exploring concepts and outcomes in Standard Assessment Tests (SATS)." *Adoption and Fostering 32*, 3, 60–72.

Davis, I. P., Lansverk, J., Newton, R., and Ganger, W. (1996) "Parental visiting and foster care reunification." *Children and Youth Services Review 18*, 363–382.

Davis-Kean, P.E. (2005) "The influence of parent education and family income on child achievement: The indirect role of parental expectations and the home environment." *Journal of Family Psychology 19*, 2, 294–304. Available at www.mikemcmahon.info/ParentEducationIncome.pdf, accessed on 6 February 2015.

Deater-Deckard, K., Petrill, S., and Thompson, L. (2007) "Anger/frustration, task persistence, and conduct problems in childhood: A behavioral genetic analysis." *J Child Psychol Psychiatry 48*, 1, 80–87.

DeGarmo, J. (2011) *Responding to the Needs of Foster Children in Rural Public Schools.* Dissertation.

dosReis, S., Zito, J., Safer, D., and Soeken, K. (2001) "Mental health services for youths in foster care and disabled youths." *American Journal of Public Health 91*, 7, 1094–1099.

Emerson, J. and Lovitt, T. (2003) "The educational plight of foster children in schools and what can be done about it." *Remedial and Special Education 24*, 4, 199–203.

Evans, E. and Armstrong, M. (1994) "Development and evaluation of treatment foster care and family-centered intensive case management in New York." *Journal of Emotional and Behavioral Disorders 2*, 4, 228–240.

Eyster, L. and Oldmixon, S.L. (2007) *State Policies to Help Youth Transition out of Foster Care.* Issue Brief. Washington, DC: NGA Center for Best Practices.

Falke, J. (1995) *Living in a Foster Home.* New York, NY: The Rosen Publishing Group, Inc.

Finkelstein, M., Wamsley, M., and Miranda, D. (2002) *What Keeps Children in Foster Care from Succeeding in School.* New York: Vera Institute of Justice.

George, R., Voorhis, J., Grant, S., Casey, K., and Robinson, M. (1992) "Special education experiences of foster children: An empirical study." *Child Welfare 71*, 5, 419–437.

Gerber, J.M. and Dicker, S. (2006) "Children adrift: Addressing the educational needs of New York's foster children." *Albany Law Review 69*, 1, 1–74.

Gilpatrick, B. (2007) "Foster kids call for the right to drive: Legal hurdles could derail a proposal intended to make it easier for foster children to obtain their driver's licenses." *Miami Herald*, 9 April.

Goelitz, G. (2007) "Answering the call to support elderly kinship carers." *15 Elder L.J. 233*, 244.

Grogan-Kaylor, A. (2000) "Who goes into foster care? The relationship of child and family characteristics to placement into kinship foster care." *Social Work Research 24*, 3, 132–141.

Halfon, N., Mendonca, A., and Berkowitz, G. (1995) "Health status of children in foster care." *Archives of Pediatric & Adolescent Medicine 140*, 386–392.

Harden, B. (2004) "Safety and stability for foster children: A developmental perspective." *The Future of Children 14*, 1, 30–47.

Hochstadt, N.J., Jaudes, P.K., Zimo, D.A., and Schachter, J. (1987) "The medical and psychosocial needs of children entering foster care." *Child Abuse and Neglect 1*, 53–62.

Horwitz, S., Owens, P., and Simms, M. (2000) "Specialized assessments for children in foster care." *Pediatrics 106*, 1, 59–66.

Howard, S. and Johnson, B. (2000) "What makes the difference? Children and teachers talk about resilient outcomes for children 'at risk'." *Educational Studies 26*, 3, 321–337.

Jackson, S. and Sachdev, D. (2001) *Better Education, Better Futures.* London, UK: Barnardo's.

Jeynes, W.H. (2005) *Parental Involvement and Student Achievement: A Meta-analysis.* Family Involvement Research Digests, December 2005. Available at www.hfrp.org/publications-resources/publications-series/family-involvement-research-digests/parental-involvement-and-student-achievement-a-meta-analysis, accessed on 6 February 2015.

Kools, S. (1999) "Self-protection in adolescents in foster care." *Journal of Child Adolescent Psychiatric Nursing 12*, 4, 139–152.

Lanier, K. personal communication, May 21, 2010.

Leslie, L., Hurlburt, M., Landsverk, J., Rolls, J., Wood, P., and Kelleher, K. (2003) "Comprehensive assessments for children entering foster care: A national perspective." *Pediatrics 112*, 1, 134–142.

Leslie, L.K., Gordon, J.N., Peoples, J., and Gist, K. (2002) "Developmental delay in young children in child welfare by initial placement type." *Infant Mental Health Journal 23*, 5, 496–516.

Lewis, L.L., Kim, Y.A., and Bey, J.A. (2011) "Teaching practices and strategies to involve inner-city parents at home and in the school." *Teaching and Teacher Education 27*, 221–234. Available at www.esev.ipv.pt/mat1Ciclo/DISCUSS%C3%95ES/Teacher%20practice.pdf, accessed on 6 February 2015.

Marcus, R. (1991) "The attachments of children in foster care." *Genetic, Social & General Psychology Monographs 117*, 41, 365–394.

Mason, A., Kosterman, R., Herrenkohl, T., Lengua, L., and McCauley, E. (2004) "Childhood conduct problems may predict depression among young adults." *Science Daily*, 12 May.

Massachusetts Society for Prevention for Cruelty to Children (2005) *18 and Out, Life After Foster Care in Massachusetts.* Boston, MA: MSPCC.

Massinga, R. and Pecora, P. (2004) "Providing better opportunities for older children in the child welfare system." *Children, Families, and Foster Care 14*, 1, 151–173.

Mata, C. (2009) "Academic achievement of foster children: Child welfare worker's perception and practices (Ed. D. dissertation)." Available from ProQuest Dissertations & Theses: Full Text (1466336).

McMillen, J.C. *et al.* (2004) "Use of mental health services among older youths in foster care." *Psychiatry Online 55*, 7, 811–817. Available at http://journals. psychiatryonline.org/article.aspx?articleid=88821, accessed on 5 February 2015.

McVey, L. and Mullis, A. (2004) "Improving the lives of children in foster care: The impact of supervised visitation." *Family Relations 53*, 293–300.

Meadowcroft, P., Thomlison, B., and Chamberlain, P. (1994) "Treatment foster care services: A research agenda for child welfare." *Child Welfare League of America 73*, 5, 565–581.

Needell, B. *et al.* (2002) *Youth Emancipating from Foster Care in California: Findings Using Linked Administrative Data.* Berkeley: Center for Social Services Research.

Parrish, T., Dubois, J., Delano, C., Dixon, C., Webster, D., and Berrick, J.D. (2001) *Education of Foster Group Home Children: Whose Responsibility is it? Study of the Educational Placement of Children Residing in Group Homes.* Palo Alto, CA: American Institute of Research.

Pecora, P., White, C., Jackson, L., and Wiggins, T. (2009) "Mental health of current and former recipients of foster care: A review of recent studies in the USA." *Child and Family Social Work 14*, 132–146.

Plotkin, C.N. (2005) "Study finds foster kids suffer PTSD." *The Harvard Crimson.* Available at www.thecrimson.com/article/2005/4/11/study-finds-foster-kids-suffer-ptsd, accessed on 5 February 2015.

Powers, P. and Stotland, J.F. (2002) *Lost in the Shuffle.* Philadelphia, PA: Education Law Center.

Purvis, K.B., Cross, D.R., and Sunshine, W.L. (2007) *The Connected Child.* New York: McGraw Hill.

Reilly, T. (2003) "Transition from care: Status and outcomes of youth who age out of foster care." *Child Welfare LXXXII*, 6, 727–747.

Sawyer, R.J. and Dubowitz, H. (1994) "School performance of children in kinship care." *Child Abuse & Neglect 18*, 587–597.

Schofield, G. and Beek, M. (2005) "Providing a secure base: Parenting children in long-term foster family care." *Attachment and Human Development 7*, 1, 3–25.

Select Committee Hearing of the California Legislature, 12 May, 2006.

Shaw, T.V., Barth, R.P., Svoboda, D.V., and Shaikh, N. (2010) *Fostering Safe Choices: Final Report.* Baltimore, MD: University of Maryland Baltimore, School of Social Work, Ruth H. Young Center for Families and Children.

Simms, M.D. (1989) "The foster care clinic: A community program to identify treatment needs of children in foster care." *Developmental & Behavioral Pediatrics 10*, 3, 121.

Simms, M., Dubowitz, H., and Szilagyi, M. (2000) "Health care needs of children in the foster care system." *Pediatrics 106*, 4, 909–918.

Smucket, K. and Kauffman, J. (1996) "School related problems of special education foster-care students with emotional or behavioral disorders: A comparison to other groups." *Journal of Emotional and Behavioral Disorders 4*, 1, 30–39.

Stahmer, A., Leslie, L., Hurlburt, M., Barth, R., Webb, M., Landsverk, J., and Zhang, J. (2005) "Development and behavioral needs and service use for young children in child welfare." *Pediatrics 116*, 4, 891–900.

Stein, E., Evans, B., Mazumdar, R., and Rae-Grant, N. (1996) "The mental health of children in foster care: A comparison with community and clinical samples." *Canadian Journal of Psychiatry 41*, 385–391.

Stephenson, C. (2009) "Turnover rate improves for child services caseworkers." *Milwaukee Journal Sentinel*, 14 September. Available at www.jsonline.com/news/milwaukee/59264702.html, accessed on 5 February 2015.

Stock, C. and Fisher, P. (2006) "Language delays among foster children: Implications for policy and practice." *Child Welfare League of America 85*, 3, 445–461.

Sullivan, A. (2009) "Teen pregnancy: An epidemic in foster care." *Time*, 22 July, 2009. Available at http://content.time.com/time/nation/article/0,8599,1911 854,00.html, accessed on 5 February 2015.

Swift, K. (2007) "A child's right: What should the state be required to provide to teenagers aging out of foster care." *William & Mary Bill of Rights Journal 15*, 4, 1207.

Takayama, J., Wolfe, E., and Coulter, K. (1998) "Relationship between reason and medical findings among children in foster care." *Pediatrics 101*, 2, 201–207.

Taussig, H., Clyman, R., and Landsverk, J. (2001) "Children who return home from foster care: A 6-year prospective study of behavioral health outcomes in adolescence." *Pediatrics 108*, 1. doi: 10.1542/peds.108.e10.

University of Connecticut (2011) "Challenges in social work today." *UCONN Today (online)*. Available at http://today.uconn.edu/blog/2011/08/challenges-in-social-work-today, accessed on 5 February 2015.

U.S. Department of Education, Office of Special Education and Rehabilitative Services, Office of Special Education Programs. (2009). *28th Annual Report to Congress on the Implementation of the Individuals with Disabilities Education Act, 2006, vol. 2*. Available at www.ed.gov/about/reports/annual/osep/2006/parts-b-c/28th-vol-2.pdf, accessed on 8 June 2015.

U.S. Department of Health and Human Services. (2010). *Foster Care Statistics, 2010*. Available at www.childwelfare.gov/pubs/factsheets/foster.cfm, accessed on 8 June 2015.

Vericker, T., Kuehn, D., & Capps, R. (2007). "Foster care placement settings and permanency planning: Patterns by child generation and ethnicity." *The Urban Institute Research of Record*. Available at www.urban.org/uploadedpdf/311459_foster_care.pdf, accessed on 8 June 2015.

Webb, M. B., Frome, P., Jones Harden, B., Baxter, R., Dowd, K., & Shin, S. H. (2007). "Addressing the educational needs of children in child welfare services." In R. Haskins, F. Wulczyn, & M. B. Webb (Eds.), *Child protection: Using research to improve policy and practice* (pp. 243–258). Washington, DC: Brookings.

Weinberg, L., Weinberg, C., & Shea, N. (1997). "Advocacy's role in identifying dysfunctions in agencies serving abused and neglected children." *Child Maltreatment, 2*, 212-225. doi:10.1177/1077559597002003004.

Weinberg, L., Zetlin, A., & Shea, N. (2003). *Improving educational prospects for foster youth*. Los Angeles, CA: Mental Health Advocacy Services, Inc.

Weinberg, L., Zetlin, A., & Shea, N. (2009). Removing barriers to education children in foster care through interagency collaboration: A seven county mulitiple-case study. *Child Welfare League of America, 88* (4), 77-111. Available at www2.americanbar.org/BlueprintForChange/Documents/weinberg2009.pdf, accessed on 8 June 2015.

Wolanin, T.R. (2005) *Higher Education Opportunities for Foster Youth*. Washington, DC: Institute for Higher Education Policy.

Wulczyn, F. (2004). "Family Reunification." *The Future of Children, 14* (1), 95-113. Available at www.futureofchildren.org/futureofchildren/publications/docs/14_01_05.pdf, accessed on 8 June 2015.

Yamamoto, Y. and Holloway, S.D. (2010) "Parental expectations and children's academic performance in sociocultural context." *Educational Psychology Review (online)*. Available at http://link.springer.com/article/10.1007/s10648-010-9121-z/fulltext.html, accessed on 6 February 2015.

Zetlin, A., Weinberg, L., & Shea, N. (2006). "Seeing the whole picture: Views from diverse participants on barriers to educating foster youths." *Children and Schools. 28* (3), 165-173.

Zima, B., Bussing, R., Freeman, S., Yang, X., Belin, T.,& Forness, S. (2000). "Behavior foster care: Their relationship to placement characteristics." *Journal of Child and Family Studies, 9* (1), 87- 10.

RESOURCES

Foster care and education

Alliance for Children's Rights

Protects the rights of impoverished, abused and neglected children and youth

http://kids-alliance.org/programs/education/education-rights-of-foster-youth

Legal Center for Foster Care and Education

www.fostercareandeducation.org

FosterParentCollege.com

Interactive multimedia training courses for adoptive, kinship, and foster parents

www.fosterparentcollege.com

Foster Care and Adoptive Community

Online training and literature

www.fosterparents.com

Court Appointed Special Advocates for Children

Educational advocacy resources

www.casaforchildren.org/site/c.mtJSJ7MPIsE/b.8346811/k.5EBE/Educational_Advocacy.htm

National Resource Center for Permanency and Family Connections

Education resources for youth in foster care

www.nrcpfc.org/is/education-and-child-welfare.html

National Center for Homeless Education

U.S. Department of Education's technical assistance and information center for the federal Education for Homeless Children and Youth (EHCY) Program

http://center.serve.org/nche

National Law Center on Homelessness & Poverty
Youth and education rights
www.nlchp.org

State of New Jersey Department of Education
Educational stability for youth in foster care
www.nj.gov/education/students/safety/edservices/stability

United Friends of the Children
Foster youth scholarships
www.unitedfriends.org/resources/links-resources/foster-youth-scholarships

Behavior management

Dr. Mac's Behavior Management Site
Positive and respectful strategies and interventions for promoting appropriate behavior
www.behavioradvisor.com

Class Dojo
Building positive behavior with students
www.classdojo.com

The Master Teacher
Techniques for managing students' behavior
www.disciplinehelp.com

Class Charts
Seating plans and behavior management
www.classcharts.com

Teacher Vision
Behavior management resources
www.teachervision.com/classroom-discipline/resource/5806.html

National Education Association
Classroom management articles and resources
www.nea.org/tools/classroom-management-articles.html

Trauma

National Child Traumatic Stress Network

Access to services for traumatized children, their families and communities throughout the United States

www.nctsn.org/resources/audiences/parents-caregivers

The National Institute for Trauma and Loss in Children

Training materials for trauma professionals

www.starr.org/training/tlc

Child Welfare Information Gateway

Trauma-Informed Practice

www.childwelfare.gov/topics/responding/trauma/

American Academy of Pediatrics and Dave Thomas Foundation for Adoption

Parenting After Trauma: Understanding your Child's Needs

www.aap.org/en-us/advocacy-and-policy/aap-health-initiatives/healthy-foster-care-america/Documents/FamilyHandout.pdf

National Resource Center for Permanency and Family Connections

Trauma-informed child welfare

www.nrcpfc.org/is/trauma-informed_child_welfare.html

American Association of Pediatrics

Healthy Foster Care America Trauma Guide

www.aap.org/en-us/advocacy-and-policy/aap-health-initiatives/healthy-foster-care-america/Pages/Trauma-Guide.aspx

National Council for Adoption

Children of Trauma: *What Educators Need to Know*

http://attachmentandintegrationmethods.com/Publications/Children_of_Trauma_2012.pdf

Aging out of care

Aging Out Institute

National resources for aging out

http://agingoutinstitute.com/general-resources

Public Broadcasting Service
Aging out resources
www.pbs.org/wnet/agingout/resources.html

Camellia Network
Connects youth aging out of foster care to the critical resources, opportunities, and support they need to thrive in adulthood
http://camellianetwork.org

The Children's Aid Society
Age-appropriate services for youth aging out of foster care
www.childrensaidsociety.org/publications/aging-out-foster-care

Foster care contact information by country

Australia
National Foster Care Association
www.fostercare.org.au/links.html

Foster Care Association of New South Wales Inc.
http://fcansw.org.au

Foster Care Association of Western Australia Inc.
www.fcawa.com.au

Foster Carer's Association of Tasmania Inc.
www.fcatas.org.au

The Foster Care Association of the ACT
(Australian Capital Territory)
www.fcaact.org.au

Foster Care Association of Victoria Inc.
www.fcav.org.au

Foster Care Queensland
www.fcq.com.au

Connecting Foster Carers SA Inc
www.cfc-sa.org.au/index.php

Foster Care Northern Territory
www.fostercarent.org.au

Canada

Canadian Foster Family Association
www.canadianfosterfamilyassociation.ca

Alberta Foster Parent Association
www.afpaonline.com

British Columbia Federation of Foster Parent Associations
www.bcfosterparents.ca

Manitoba Foster Family Network
www.mffn.ca

New Brunswick Family and Community Services
www2.gnb.ca/content/gnb/en/departments/social_development.html

Newfoundland & Labrador Foster Families Association
www.nlffa.ca

Foster Family Coalition of the Northwest Territories
www.ffcnwt.com

Foster Parents Society of Ontario
www.fosterparentssociety.org

Durham Foster Parent Association
www.durhamfpa.com/page/page/4711854.htm

Fédération des familles d'accueil du Québec
www.ffaq.ca

Saskatchewan Foster Families Association
www.sffa.sk.ca

United Kingdom

The Fostering Network
England
87 Blackfriars Road
London SE1 8HA
Phone: 020 7620 6400
Fax: 020 7620 6401
Website: www.fostering.net
Email: info@fostering.net

Northern Ireland
Unit 10
40 Montgomery Road
Belfast BT6 9HL
Phone: 028 9070 5056
Fax: 028 9079 9215
Website: www.fostering.net
Email: ni@fostering.net

Scotland
Ingram House
2nd floor
227 Ingram Street
Glasgow G1 1DA
Phone: 0141 204 1400
Fax: 0141 204 6588
Website: www.fostering.net
Email: scotland@fostering.net

Wales
1 Caspian Point
Pierhead Street
Cardiff Bay
CF10 4DQ
Phone: 029 2044 0940
Fax: 029 2044 0941
Website: www.fostering.net
Email: wales@fostering.net

United States of America
National Foster Parent Association
National Foster Parent Association
1202 Westrac Drive, Suite 400
Fargo, ND 58103
Phone: 800-557-5238
Fax: 888-925-5634
Webiste: http://nfpaonline.org
Email: Info@NFPAonline.org

Alabama Department of Human Resources
Center for Communications
Gordon Persons Building, Suite 2104
50 North Ripley Street
Montgomery, AL 36130
Phone: 334 242-1310
Website: http://dhr.alabama.gov/services/Foster_Care/FC_Children_Teens.
aspx

Alaska Health and Social Services
350 Main Street, Room 404
PO Box 110601
Juneau, Alaska 99811-0601
Phone: (907) 465-3030
Website: http://dhss.alaska.gov/ocs/Pages/FosterCare/default.aspx

Arkansas Foster Family Services
P.O. Box 1437, Slot S560
Little Rock, AR, 72203-1437
Phone: 501-682-1442
Website: www.fosterarkansas.org

Arizona Division of Children, Youth, and Families
P.O. Box 6123 Site Code 940A
Phoenix, AZ 85007
Phone: 877-543-7633
Website: www.azdes.gov/az_adoption

California Department of Social Services
744 P Street
Sacramento, CA 95814
Phone: 916- 651-8788
Website: www.cdss.ca.gov/cdssweb/Default.htm

Colorado Department of Human Services
1575 Sherman Street, 1st Floor
Denver, CO 80203-1714
Phone: 1-800-799-5876
Website:www.colorado.gov/cs/Satellite/CDHS-Main/CBON/125157508
3520

Connecticut Department of Children and Families
Commissioner's Office
505 Hudson Street
Hartford, CT 06106
Phone: 860-550-6300
Website: www.mi.gov/dhs/0,4562,7-124-9202-144763--,00.html

Delaware Services for Children, Youth, and their Families
1825 Faulkland Road,
Wilmington, DE 19805
Phone: 302-451-2800
Website: http://kids.delaware.gov/fs/fostercare.shtml

District of Columbia Child and Family Services Agency
400 6th Street, SW
Washington, DC 20024
Phone: 202-442-6100
Email: cfsa@dc.gov

Florida Department of Children and Families
100 Opa-locka Boulevard
Opa-locka, FL 33054
Phone: (305) 769-6324
Website: www.fosteringflorida.com/index.shtml

Georgia Department of Family and Children Services
2 Peachtree Street, NW
Suite 18-486
Atlanta, Georgia 30303
Phone: 404-651-9361
Website: http://dfcs.dhs.georgia.gov/portal/site/DHS-DFCS

Hawaii Department of Human Services
Hui Ho'omalu
680 Iwilei Road, Suite 500
Honolulu, HI 96817
Phone: 1-888-879-8970
Website: http://hawaii.gov/dhs/protection/social_services/child_welfare/
Foster

Idaho Department of Health and Welfare
PO Box 83720
Boise, ID 83720-0036
Phone: 800-926-2588
Website: www.healthandwelfare.idaho.gov/Children/AdoptionFosterCare
Home/tabid/75/Default.aspx

Illinois Department of Family and Children Services
406 East Monroe Street
Springfield, Illinois 62701
Phone: 1-800-572-2390
Website: www.state.il.us/dcfs/foster/index.shtml

Indiana Department of Child Services
953 Monument Drive
Lebanon, IN 46052
Phone: 1-888-631-9510
Website: www.in.gov/dcs/index.htm

Iowa Department of Human Services
1305 E. Walnut,
Des Moines, IA 50319-0114
Phone: 515-281-5521
Website: www.dhs.iowa.gov

Kansas Department for Children and Families
230 E. William
Wichita, KS 67201
Phone: 785-296-4653
Website: www.srs.ks.gov/agency/Pages/AgencyInformation.aspx

Kentucky Cabinet for Health and Family Services
Office of the Secretary
275 E. Main St.
Frankfort, KY 40621
Phone: 1-800-372-2973
Website: http://chfs.ky.gov

Louisiana Department of Children and Family Services
627 N. Fourth St.
Baton Rouge, LA 70802
Phone: 888-524-3578
Website: www.dss.state.la.us

Maine Office of Child and Family Services
2 Anthony Avenue
Augusta, Me 04333-0011
Phone: 207-624-7900
Website: www.maine.gov/dhhs/ocfs

Maryland Department of Human Services
311 West Saratoga St.
Baltimore, MD 21201
Phone: 410-767-7130
Website: www.dhr.state.md.us/blog

Massachusetts Department of Children and Families
24 Farnsworth St.
Boston, MA 02210
Phone: 617-348-8400
Website: www.mass.gov/eohhs/gov/departments/dcf

Michigan Department of Human Services
Department of Human Services
235 S. Grand Ave. P.O. Box 30037 Lansing, Michigan 48909
Phone: 1-866-540-0008
Website: www.mi.gov/dhs/0,4562,7-124-60126---,00.html

Minnesota Department of Human Services
PO Box 64244
St. Paul, MN 55164-0244
Phone: 651-431-3830
Website: http://mn.gov/dhs

Missouri Department of Social Services
Broadway State Office Building
P.O. Box 1527
Jefferson City, MO 65102-1527
Phone: 573-751-4815
Website: www.dss.mo.gov/cd/fostercare

Mississippi Department of Human Services
750 N. State St.
Jackson, MS 39202
Phone: 601-359-4500
Website: www.mdhs.state.ms.us

Nebraska Division of Children and Family Services
P.O. Box 95026
Lincoln, NE 68509-5044
Phone: (402) 471-9272
Website: http://dhhs.ne.gov/publichealth/Pages/chs_foc_focindex.aspx

Nevada Division of Child and Family Services
4126 Technology Way, 3rd Floor
Carson City, NV 89706
Phone: 775-684-4400
Website: http://dcfs.state.nv.us

New Hampshire Department of Health and Human Services
129 Pleasant St.
Concord, NH 03301-3852
Phone: 800-894-5533
Website: www.dhhs.nh.gov/dcyf/index.htm

New Jersey Department of Children and Families
20 West State Street, 4th floor
PO Box 729
Trenton, NJ 08625-0729
Phone: 877-652-0729
Website: www.state.nj.us/dcf/index.shtml

New Mexico Children, Youth, and Families Department
P.O. Drawer 5160
Santé Fe, MN 87502-5160
Phone: 800-432-2075
Website: www.cyfd.org

New York Office of Children and Family Services
52 Washington St.
Renssleaer, NY 12144-2736
Phone: 518-473-7793
Website: http://ocfs.ny.gov

North Carolina Department of Health and Human Services
2001 Mail Service Center
Raleigh, NC 27699-2001
Phone: 919-855-4800
Website: www.ncdhhs.gov/childrenandyouth/index.htm

North Dakota Department of Children and Family Services
600 East Boulevard Avenue Department 325
Bismarck ND 58505-0250
Phone: 701-328-2316
Website: www.nd.gov/dhs/services/childfamily

Ohio Department of Jobs and Family Services
30 E. Broad Street, 32nd Floor
Columbus, Ohio 43215
Phone: 614-466-1213
Website: http://jfs.ohio.gov/

Oklahoma Department of Human Services
Sequoyah Memorial Office Building
2400 N. Lincoln Blvd.
Oklahoma City, OK 73105
Phone: 1-800-376-9729
Website: www.okdhs.org

Oregon Department of Human Services
500 Summer St. NE E62
Salem, OR 97301-1067
Phone: 503-945-5944
Website: www.oregon.gov/DHS/children

Pennsylvania Department of Public Welfare
625 Forster Street
Harrisburg, PA 17120
Phone: 800-692-7462
Website: www.dhs.state.pa.us

Rhode Island Department of Human Services
Louis Pasteur Building #57
600 New London Avenue
Cranston, RI 02920
Phone: 401-462-2121
Website: www.dhs.ri.gov

South Carolina Department for Children and Families
P.O. Box 1520
Columbia, SC 29202-1520
Phone: 803-898-7601
Website: https://dss.sc.gov/content/customers/index.aspx

South Dakota Department of Social Services
700 Governors Drive
Pierre, SD 57501
Phone: 605-773-3165
Website: https://dss.sd.gov/

Tennessee Department of Children's Services
Cordell Hull Building, 7th Floor
Nashville, TN 37243
Phone: 615-741-9701
Website: www.state.tn.us/youth

Texas Department of Family and Protective Services
701 W. 51st St
Austin, TX 78751
Phone: 1-800-233-3405
Website: www.dfps.state.tx.us

Utah Department of Child and Family Services
195 North 1950 West
Salt Lake City, Utah 84116
Phone: 801-538-4100
Website: www.dcfs.utah.gov

Vermont Department for Children and Families
103 South Main Street, 2 & 3 North
Waterbury, VT 05671-5500
Phone: 800-649-2642
Website: http://dcf.vermont.gov

Virginia Department of Social Services
801 E. Main Street
Richmond, VA 23219-2901
Phone: 800-468-8894
Website: www.dss.virginia.gov/family/fc/index.cgi

Washington Department of Social and Health Services
PO Box 45130
Olympia, WA 98504-5130
Phone: 800-737-0617
Website: www.dshs.wa.gov/ca/general/index.asp

West Virginia Children and Family Services
350 Capitol Street, Room 691
Charleston, West Virginia 253013704
Phone: 304-558-3431
Website: www.wvdhhr.org/bcf/children_adult/foster

Wisconsin Department of Children and Families
201 East Washington Avenue, Second Floor
P.O. Box 8916
Madison, WI 53708-8916
Phone: 608-267-3905
Website: http://dcf.wisconsin.gov

Wyoming Department of Family Services
2451 Foothill Blvd., Suite 103
Rock Springs, WY 82901
Phone: 307-352-2509
Website: http://dfsweb.state.wy.us/protective-services/foster-care/index.
html

ABOUT THE AUTHOR

Dr. John DeGarmo has been a foster parent since 2001, and he and his wife have had over 45 children come through their home. Dr. DeGarmo wrote his dissertation on fostering, entitled *Responding to the Needs of Foster Children in Rural Schools*. He is a speaker and trainer on many topics about the foster care system, and travels across the nation delivering passionate, dynamic, energetic, and informative presentations. Dr. DeGarmo is the author of the highly inspirational and bestselling books *Fostering Love: One Foster Parent's Story*, *Keeping Foster Children Safe Online*, *The Foster Parenting Manual: A Practical Guide to Creating a Loving, Safe, and Stable Home*, and the foster care children's book *A Different Home: A New Foster Child's Story*. He also writes for a number of publications and newsletters, both in the UK and in the United States, and overseas. He is married to Dr. Kelly DeGarmo, and the two of them are the parents of six children, both biological and adopted. In his spare time, he enjoys gardening, traveling, and performing. He is currently located in the United States, in Georgia. Dr. DeGarmo can be contacted by email at drjohndegarmo@gmail, through his Facebook page, Dr. John DeGarmo, or at his website, http://drjohndegarmofostercare. weebly.com.

INDEX